FIRENZE
MVSEI

P R O F I L I

1

© 2000   Ministero per i Beni e le Attività Culturali -
Soprintendenza per i Beni Artistici e Storici di Firenze, Pistoia e Prato

A publication of
s i l l a b e s.r.l.
Livorno
www.sillabe.it

iconographic research and captions: *Ilaria Taddei*
managing editor: *Maddalena Paola Winspeare*
graphic design: *Gianluigi Guarnotta*
editing: *Bettina Müller*
translation: *Richard Fowler*

fotographs: *Archivio Sillabe: Foto Remo Bardazzi, Foto Paolo Nannoni*
                     Archivio Fotografico SBAA *Firenze, Archivio Fotografico* SBAS *Firenze,*
                     Archivio Mandragora, Giuseppe d'Abruzzo, Nicolò Orsi Battaglini

photolitography: *La Nuova Lito - Firenze; Studio Lito - Città di Castello*

ISBN 88-8347-053-2

Massimo Winspeare

THE MEDICI

THE GOLDEN AGE
OF COLLECTING

sillabe

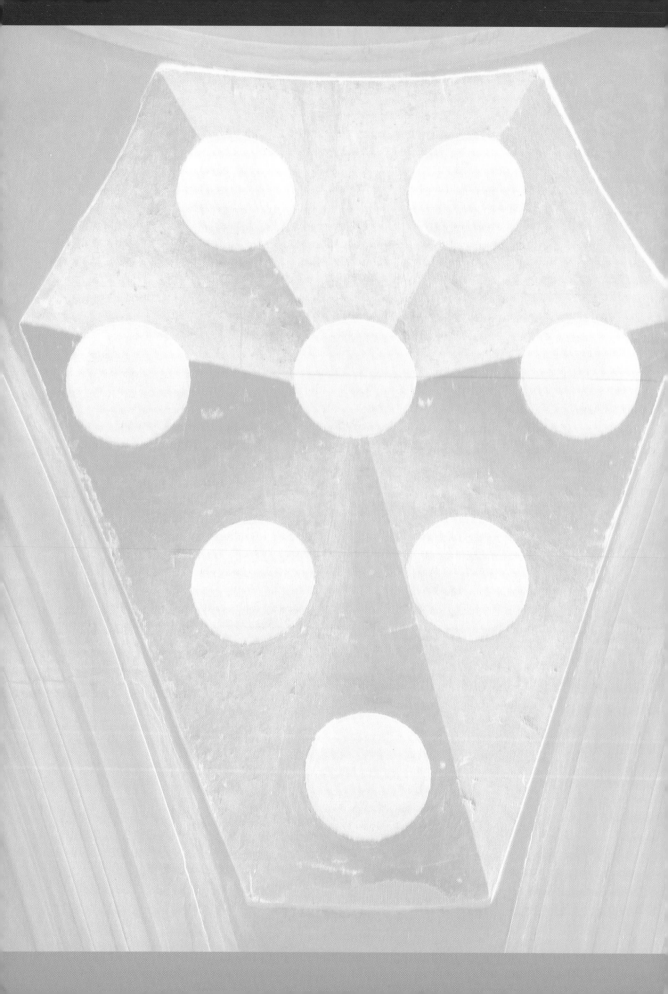

Contents

BERNARDO DADDI STUDIO, *Madonna of Mercy*, detail, 1342, Florence, Bigallo Museum

FLORENCE
BEFORE
THE MEDICI

It still seems to be difficult precisely to define Florence's beginnings because the effective date of its appearance in the chronicles of art, finance and war is confused with that of its acquisition of an identity of its own corresponding to indisputable independence and political liberty. This brief look at the magnificent story of the city will take an outline of certain events from the first two centuries of its history as its point of reference. It will make the beginning of Florence coincide with the period following the death of Countess Matilde (1115) and more precisely with the period around 1182. It was in 1182 that, control having been taken of Pogna, the Florentine Consuls were named with certainty for the first time as representatives of the will of the Commune, established and recognised as such. It is from this point on that the question of a city-state concerns us.

We will therefore not refer to the dispute (which remains, moreover, unresolved) concerning the reliability of the legend of Florence's true origins, since the legend has so many versions that it frankly seems that each one is a unique legend of its own. These versions do, however, all have a common denominator: the suggestion that it was Fiesole, the most beautiful and most wholesome city in Europe at the time (its name deriving from *fie sola*), that gave birth to Florence. How and why this came about seem to be part of the fables, of the myth, that do not concern us. It suffices here to recall that Florence already existed at the time of ancient Rome, when it was known as *Florentia* and was considered by Caesar to be one of his colonies. Later, after the fall of the Empire and during the wars which broke out all over Europe, with Italy as their tragic background, the city continued to develop its own commercial interests, proving itself to be precocious in this regard, reconciling the affairs of the Republic with the growth of its economy. The city recovered so effectively and successfully that, in the second half of the twelfth century, it became the most flourishing Commune in Tuscany. It surpassed Lucca (the capital of the marquisate) with its leadership, and became more powerful than Pisa and Siena, the former a natural port and an outlet for Florence's thriving foreign commerce, the latter its historical rival.

As is always the case, the stimulating effects of economic development and the power of capital worked well together, and the city prospered. If success depends on good organisation, this may explain the surprising results the city achieved.

Florence very quickly established plans, rules and discipline such as to guarantee it extraordinary efficiency and absolute competitiveness in its territorial context.

GIOTTO,
Funeral Rites of St. Francis,
circa 1325,
Florence, Santa Croce,
Bardi Chapel

MINO DA FIESOLE,
Monument to Marquis Ugo di Toscana,
1469-1481, Florence,
Badia Fiorentina (Benedictine Abbey)

Florence went through a period of economic and political recovery at the end of the 10th century. This revival was due to Marquis Ugo di Toscana, who governed the city as Emperor Othon III's vicar. His remains, which are honoured still today, are kept in the Badia Fiorentina founded by his mother Willa.

In the economic life of the Middle Ages, industrial activity was variously formulated, with prevalence given to personal improvisation, but in Florence it was decided to give such activity a corporate structure that became the very basis of its way of operating. Banks and bankers improved the system, stimulating it and creating that virtuous spiral so dear to today's economists. Thirteenth-century Florence was already surpassing every other city, not only in Italy but also in all of Europe, in the manufacture of refined and sought-after goods and in the skill with which they were produced. Moreover, it had the moral, intellectual, creative and economic resources that are indispensable for any kind of successful competition.

All of this also derived from the fact that, since its beginnings, Florence had had a high concentration of exceptional people, with Roman origins and traditions, who were mainly artisans but who also had the habit of establishing small, original family businesses characterised by esprit de corps and a strong sense of creativity.

At first, these people had to struggle with the difficulties inherent in managing their businesses in the absence of an appropriately regulatory government. Very little is in fact known about the constitutional origins of Florentine government in general.

During this time, Matilde di Canossa, the daughter of Bonifacio, the marquis of Tuscany, ought to have taken at least some interest in Florentine affairs but preferred instead to become involved in foreign politics, intervening in the struggle for investitures and taking on the role of supporter of the Pope's sovereignty.

When she died, on July 4th 1115, Matilde made the Church her only heir.

View of the Bardi Chapel,
Florence, Santa Croce

*The Bardi were powerful
Florentine bankers with
branches throughout Europe.
They loaned considerable sums
of money to Edward III of
England, who was engaged in
a war against France. To the
glory of God, and especially to
that of their own name, they
became the patrons of a chapel
in Santa Croce and asked
Giotto to fresco it.*

At the time, the people of Florence were surrounded by hostile nobility, of predominantly Germanic origin, who remained outside the city walls, having no need to enter non-strategic territory. Florence, in fact, was not spread out across a plain, like Pisa and Lucca, nor protected on a mountain like Siena and Arezzo, but lay in a valley, in the midst of a circle of enclosing hills. It was as if the city was surrounded, vulnerable to being oppressed and harassed by potential enemies who could, whenever they liked, control the exit routes that were indispensable for the city's commercial activity. The need and desire to survive and to maintain comfortable economic well-being, gained with the qualities described above, along with the need to provide for its own defence in the struggle against the Empire, led the Florentines to organise themselves even before the Commune had a defined and officially recognised existence. It did this by means of the associations, the companies, and the groups into which the citizens divided themselves and which they organised. These groups soon became significantly visible and powerful, under the names of the Major and Minor Guilds.

In the absence of Matilde, felt also in the conduct of trials and courts, the administration of justice was carried out by judges on their own. This in fact became the precursory sign of the city's independence, before the Commune had yet acquired its true autonomy. While this was taking place within the context of the community (organised according to a plan which we will examine shortly), the political and military importance reached by Florence was made manifest in its hegemony over the League formed by the three Tuscan cities as an anti-imperial move, in San Genesio in 1197. However, in order to exercise a legitimate predominance on the foreign level, it was necessary to be internally strong. And Florence was strong, with the support of its formidable corporations, the Guilds.

There were seven Major Guilds: judges and notaries, merchants who refined foreign cloth, moneychangers, wool merchants, silk merchants, physicians and herbalists, squirrel-furriers and furriers.

The Minor Guilds, of which there were fourteen, included butchers, shoemakers, blacksmiths, woodworkers and stonemasons, linen merchants and second-hand dealers, keysmiths and ironworkers, oil merchants, salami and cheese merchants, strap merchants, leather merchants and sandal makers, armour- and swordmakers, lumber merchants, wine merchants, innkeepers, and bakers. The textile and moneychanger guilds were for a long time the most powerful, partly because they developed more quickly than the others did.

In 1252, Florence's influence on world economy culminated with the creation of its own coin, the florin, which, in the general confusion of the monetary market of the time, became an important unit of measure in Europe and even in some countries in North Africa. The florin was symbolic of a growth that had seen Florence expand beyond the ancient Roman walls, with houses, factories and artisan workshops. It was symbolic of an economic development brilliantly achieved by prosperous people who, after the death of Frederick II, in 1250, had rebelled against the magnates, seizing the Commune and installing the government of the *First People*.

The Ghibellini, defenders of the aristocratic citizens, who, while Frederick II was alive had dominated Florence, were thus removed by the

MASOLINO,
*Recovery of the Lame Man and
Resurrection of Tabita*,
1424-1425, Florence,
Santa Maria del Carmine,
Brancacci Chapel

National Bargello Museum, Florence

*Constructed in the middle of the 13th
century as the premises for the People's
Captain. It was thus the first building
built specifically to house civic
institutions.*

Guelphs, representatives of the interests of the manufacturing and mercantile classes. The defeated exiles refused, however, to give in and, with the help of Manfredi, defeated the Guelphs at Montaperti in 1260 and, returned to Florence, took control of the Commune once again.

But the antagonism of nearby centres, most of which were controlled by the Ghibellini, gave the city an additional motive for claiming its own autonomous identity, so that, on the death of Manfredi in 1266, and after the collapse of the Swabians in Tagliacozzo in 1268, it once more passed into the hands of the Guelphs, with a government that was called the *Second People*.

From this point on, merchants and bankers, their power strengthened, excluded the magnates from the magistracies and, widening the social base, brought representatives of the medium-sized and minor Guilds into the government. By means of elaborate agreements concluded in 1293-1294 with Giano della Bella's *Legal Code*, the noble families and magnates were excluded from access to any political role whatsoever.

With these values, the significance of which the parties concerned were perhaps not immediately aware, the constitutional principle of the supremacy of Florentine merchants and bankers, who would become the real future protagonists in the developing story of the city, was established.

Unfortunately, however, these were times of great uncertainty and instability within all the European political and institutional structures. It was thus inevitable that populations within individual states would take sides for the defence of their own advantages or ideals, with the unavoidable consequence that divisions were created that were so marked as to become actual factions or parties.

In Florence, at the beginning of the fourteenth century, the Guelph movement split into the *White* and *Black* parties. The former, led by the Cerchi family, was supported by the rich bourgeois and by representatives of the Minor Guilds; the latter, led by the Donati family, was based in the ecclesiastical hierarchies and sought the restoration of the aristocracy. This feud, in spite of an initial victory by the Blacks, did not have the hoped-for success, and the Major Guilds remained in power.

In 1300-1301, there was a sudden foreign intervention by Pope Boniface VIII (1235-1303), who sent Charles of Valois to Florence to support the Black

Orsanmichele, Florence

*Symbol of the power of the Guilds,
who decorated the exterior
walls with niches for their patron saints.*

Palazzo Vecchio (Old Palace), Florence

*Seat of political power from the time it was
built, the palace was constructed at the end
of the 13th century as premises for the
Priors and the Gonfalonier.*

faction and to help it prevail. The Blacks were partisans of the Church and had members among the highest aristocracy, who, having moved on from their agrarian interests, were mainly financiers, bankers and merchants. In any case, the passage of Charles through Florence left hardly a trace.

Henry VII, who had designs on Florence in 1311-1312, posed more of a risk, but, faced with the danger he represented for them, the Florentines closed ranks and behaved in a particularly militant manner. They even incited the Brescians, who were being attacked by Henry, to resist fiercely and decisively, stimulating the Perugians to shake off the yoke of the invader, and to recover their dignity and freedom. The Florentines carried out an aggressive propaganda program that was astute and that served their own interests.

In addition, as a confirmation of their expedient, if also opportunistic, unitarian spirit, on September 2 1311, with an act of reconciliation that was called the *Baldo d'Aguglione Reform*, they brought back to the city all those who could be considered friends of the Guelphs. They confirmed the banishment of only the unyielding Ghibellini. Dante was not among those who returned, as he was judged to be too dangerous.

Henry VII sent two new ambassadors to the city who, completely unwanted, were in danger of coming to a bad end: robbed, their lives threatened, they were convinced by more moderate of the city's politicians to return to where they had come from.

Following this, because of having angered and offended the Emperor, whose requests for an apology it ignored, Florence was banished from the Empire (1312).

Nevertheless, Florence's reaction was strong and decisive. Significant evidence of the straightforwardness and strength of character of the hard and pragmatic Florentine people is found in the correspondence that some of the city's leaders sent to the King of France. Stimulated by the worrying necessity of conducting international affairs and of seeing to the city's development even during the war, they wrote to the King asking that he ensure that their commerce could continue without interruption. In order to make their request more convincing, they painted a dramatic picture of Henry's aggression, expressing themselves in a way that was intended to win the King's sympathy, while at the same time describing the serious disadvantages that his aggression was creating for them.

But, in a move characteristic of the alternating events of an unsettled and indefinite international context, the Ghibellini, following the arrival in Italy of Henry VII (1310-1313) and then of Ludwig of Bavaria (1327-1329), inflicted two severe defeats on the Florentines: at Montecatini, led by Uguccione della Faggiola (1315) and at Altopascio (1325), under Castruccio Castracani. Florence consequently lost a part of its independence.

There followed dark years during which the city was ruled by Carlo, Duke of Calabria, although it did have some success with troops sent abroad by the Commune, conquering Pistoia (1331), Cortona (1332), Arezzo (1337) and Colle Val d'Elsa (1338). These successful undertakings at least made it possible for Florence to regain supremacy in Tuscany.

The city's decline continued under the brief despotism of Gualtieri di Brienne, Duke of Athens. This was a period which today would be described

as one of reflection of and of the city turning inwards towards itself, at the end of which there occurred two events that are dissimilar but equally relevant to the city's history.

The first was the war against Gregory XI conducted by the merchants who, even though they were confirmed Guelphs, and had many commercial interests in Rome, were ready to fight against the Pope when he threatened their freedom. They did so with particular determination, significantly defining *Eight Saints*, the magistrates responsible for leading the war of the same name. In fact, Gregory, reinstating papal authority in Romagna, had created among the Florentines the uncomfortable and detestable feeling of being surrounded and their reaction was therefore justified.

The second event, completely internal, was the Riot of the Wool Workers, the wool carders, which took place on July 21 1378. The rebellion was the consequence of the exasperation of these humble workers with the miserable compensation they received for their work and with their total dependence on the wool corporation, which, by means of severe restrictions, had made their existence very difficult. The immediate result of the revolt was the breaking of the nobles' power and the destruction of the Guelphs' oligarchy. The rebels, along with the minor Guilds, seized the Commune and opened the city's magistracy to all the Guilds, including the newly created People of God Guilds.

The new Doublet Makers Guild included barbers, tailors, clippers and doublet makers; the Dyers Guild included those who belonged to the Wool and Silk Guilds; the Wool Workers, or common people's, Guild included minor wool workers, apprentice dyers, weavers and combers.

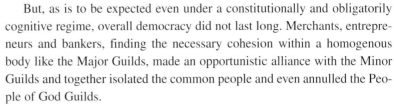

PAOLO UCCELLO,
Equestrian monument to Giovanni Acuto,
1436, Florence, Duomo (Cathedral)

*The famous English condottiere
fought in the pay
of the Florentine Republic
from 1377 to 1394,
the year of his death.*

But, as is to be expected even under a constitutionally and obligatorily cognitive regime, overall democracy did not last long. Merchants, entrepreneurs and bankers, finding the necessary cohesion within a homogenous body like the Major Guilds, made an opportunistic alliance with the Minor Guilds and together isolated the common people and even annulled the People of God Guilds.

It was in these very years that a Medici appeared on the scene, even if in a somewhat hidden role: Giovanni di Bicci.

He was the son of Averardo, nicknamed Bicci, a descendent of a family that on various occasions had played an important role in the people's struggle against the magnates. It even seems that in 1378 a distant relative, a cousin of his grandfather, Salvestro de' Medici, had been one of the organisers of the riots. Giovanni, a member of the Moneychangers Guild and a socially visible man, discerning and esteemed, remained to a certain extent antagonistic to the nobles.

He was the true founder of a powerful family but was always attentive, even in later years, to the people's cause. He was capable of setting up the infrastructure for and supporting the development of a republic which came to be universally recognised as the "most republican republic that the world had ever seen". In fact, with its system of government, Florence produced what was at the time proportionally the most numerous and most aware political class in Europe. This corresponded to reality also from the merely statistical point of view. It is sufficient to consider that out of an overall population of around fifty thousand people (around sixty thousand before the plagues of 1348 and a little more than forty thousand after), five or six thousand individuals were able to hold office, in rotation. For this reason, it was not easy for power to be concentrated in the hands of a few and even less easy for it to be controlled by one person.

During the long period which preceded the entrance of the Medici family into the history of Florence, a period characterised by the wars between the Empire and the Papacy, with their inevitable consequences on the city's overall economic situation and with the internal upheavals that they had aggravated, the Florentines had occupied themselves in other directions as well. They paid attention to the growth of their own city and its territorial development, and realised architectural, sculptural, pictorial and literary works that, even though only of moderate significance with respect to the other politically engaged Guilds, were a definite expression of the Fine or Liberal Arts, that is, Arts in the strict sense of the word (The Italian word "Arte" translates into English as "Guild" when used to mean "corporation" or "association").

Two individuals stood out over all the others and distinguished themselves in the Fine Arts as true geniuses: Giotto and Dante, architect and poet respectively. They directly influenced the culture of a people sensitive to well-being and to beauty, to what, that is, would today be called "the quality of life". To these two giants must be added the name of Giovanni Boccacci, better known as Boccaccio. His intellectual gifts were not on the same level as theirs, but he was equally great when it came to spirit and innovation.

Let us take a closer look at them.

GIOTTO

(VESPIGNANO DEL MUGELLO, 1267? - FLORENCE, 1337)

Like all true innovators, Giotto was not immediately understood as having modified the aesthetic canons to which people had by now become accustomed. His intellectual contemporary, Boccaccio, on the other hand, crediting Giotto with the rebirth of painting, was gratified that Giotto did not follow the fashion of the times, in that he was consistent in contributing more to pleasure for the eyes than intellectual stimulation. This was an appreciation for the culture of an artist who, initially inspired by sculpture, which had evolved further in the recovery of classical values, was able to break away from it, widening and extending his means of expression beyond what the sculptors themselves had been able to do.

This resulted in painting acquiring universal values because of Giotto's manifest ability to represent, by means of a specific language, every aspect of reality, developing a new iconography endowed with original themes.

If this is the critical aspect of his pictorial revolution, the historical evaluation appears to be even more pertinent to a reflection on Humanism, which seems to anticipate Renaissance values. Giotto, placing man at the centre of the imagined situation with the intent of making him the fulcrum around which to render reality plausible and earthly, abandoned the modes of Greek and Byzantine art, reacquiring the values of Latin classicism. Struck by this new way of proposing images, Vasari, in expressing his opinion on the artistic upheavals taking place at the time, used a term that would define, from then on, a precise historical period: "The art of drawing had in Tuscany, or better, in Florence itself, its own Renaissance". On the basis of these aesthetic foundations, Giotto's objective was to form –

Giotto's bell tower, Florence

GIOTTO,
Ognissanti Madonna,
circa 1310, Florence, Uffizi

and he succeeded in doing so – as homogeneous a school as possible, which would make it possible for him to express his ideas, on panels or frescoes. The result was so concretely brilliant that it led to the flourishing of artists defined as "Giottoesque", sometimes repetitive but always of excellent quality, and who made the name *of their founder into a sort of trademark guarantee of particularly high pictorial quality.*

In Florence, the master's art was expressed, as both architect and painter, in the design of the Carraia Bridge (destroyed during the Second World War), in the magnificent bell tower of the Duomo (Cathedral), in the pictorial cycles in the Peruzzi and Badri chapels in the Santa Croce Church, as well as in various panel paintings, among which mention will only be made here of the Ognisanti Madonna *and the extraordinary Santa Maria Novella* Crucifix, *a definitive departure from the preceding pictorial tradition.*

Dante Alighieri
(Florence, 1265 – Ravenna, 1321)

From the time of his youth, the greatest of the Italian poets undertook to use the vernacular, which he wanted to raise to the level of a true poetic language. He skilfully experimented with it in the Dolce stil nuovo compositions and then used it, rendering it sublime, in the absolute masterpiece of poetry of all time: The Divine Comedy.

And yet, the man who was able to create such art lived at the mercy of political vicissitudes that only the uncertainty and confusion of the time could provoke. Although he was excluded from political activity until 1295 because of the Legal Code, he came to the attention of the Florentines by means of the use of a provision that made it necessary for anyone who wanted to work in a Guild to be registered as a member. He chose the Physicians and Herbalists Guild. His introduction into city government was relatively easy and he held various offices between 1295 and 1302. He belonged to the Council of the One Hundred (1296) and also became one of the Priors (1300). In this capacity, he contributed to the banishment of the quarrelsome leaders of the White and Black factions, even though his great friend Guido Cavalcanti belonged to the former.

Even though he was opposed to the Pope's unscrupulous moral and political behaviour, he was sent with two other ambassadors to the court of Boniface VIII. His mission companions were allowed to return freely, but Dante never again set foot in Florence.

In fact, he was condemned in absentia in 1302 and exiled. He was discouraged from returning on the explicit threat of being killed by the Blacks, who had taken power in the meantime. After various wanderings, Dante ended up living in Ravenna, where finally he died, at the court of Guido da Polenta. As with Giotto, it is not our task here to detail the Master's works, which are now part of our universal cultural heritage.

BEATO ANGELICO, *Universal Judgement*, detail, circa 1425, Florence, San Marco Museum

GIOVANNI BOCCACCIO
(FLORENCE?, 1313 – CERTALDO, 1375)

VINCENZO CABIANCA,
The Florentine Storytellers,
1861, Florence, Pitti Palace,
Gallery of Modern Art

Boccaccio was the son of a merchant from Certaldo who, in 1317, became consul of the Moneychangers Guild, which was connected to the powerful Bardi family. His interesting missions led him to travel considerably. He visited Paris, a city with which the Florentines had intense business relationships, on several occasions. His father's profession explains why an individual like Giovanni, who was clearly not adept at practical matters, was nevertheless introduced into social life as an expert in the art of commerce and sent to work for a commercial enterprise in Naples. It was there that, in 1331, he met Madonna Fiammetta, a meeting which gave him the opportunity to leave the world of business behind and to dedicate himself to the world of letters.

While the distance between Boccaccio's life and the world of poetry was not as great as was the case for Dante and Petrarch, it may still be said that his most well known (and, in all senses of the word, most criticised) work, the Decameron, was of the highest literary value. Its scabrous themes, which he treated with exemplary spirit and elegance that temper the realistic crudeness that would otherwise risk seeming vulgar, were redeemed by tight formal control of the narrative range, according to classical patterns of a kind that became defined as the humanism of the vernacular. On the other hand, the rediscovery and study of classical texts, which were at the roots of Renaissance humanism, may rightly be considered the source of Boccaccio's literary personality, as was also the case with his great friend Petrarch, whose most famous works confirm his humanistic roots.

Among Boccaccio's most important works are: Filoloco, Filostrato, Bucolicum Carmen, De casibus deorum illustrorum, De claris mulieribus, and De genealogis deorum, which was an extensive encyclopaedia of ancient mythology and on which he worked until his death.

He also had important public responsibilities, as in 1365 when he acted as ambassador for Urban V. He travelled to Genoa, Nice and Avignon, where he met Petrarch's last surviving friends. Among his various missions in 1367, he organised a journey to Venice where he hoped to meet his great friend, but managed to greet only Petrarch's daughter Francesca.

In 1370, he returned to Naples. In 1373, probably while he was staying at Certaldo, he was invited to Florence to give a public reading of The Comedy in the Santo Stefano Church. This invitation was an official recognition of his skill as a performer but was also a confirmation of the peace he had made with Dante, who had become quite famous, assimilating the latter's superior poetic values for the enrichment of the culture of a vigorous people.

He died in 1375, on December 31, at Certaldo.

Medici coat of arms, cupola of the Sagrestia Vecchia (Old Sacristy), Florence, San Lorenzo

THE RISE OF THE MEDICI FAMILY

In a city as lively and as participatory as Florence, populated by people who were distinguished by the particular arts of making beautiful objects or of formulating ideas tending to improve existence, an autonomous form of cultural behaviour grew up, often in rebellion against any form of coercion that attempted to change the behaviour the society had deliberately taken on and made its own.

In this context, it was easy for one individual to stand out from the others and, in the transition from professional success to economic conquest, unprecedented competition grew up. In order to avoid anarchy in the use of these resources, regulations were needed. Florence, for the reasons already mentioned, was a city of individualists. In order to avoid the consequences of destructive competition among them, they had no recourse other than to keep an eye on one another. And this could only occur by means of widespread and strict, control and self-control mechanisms, at the summit of which there was extremely frequent turnover.

In this climate, thanks to its profitable activity in the Moneychangers Guild, the Medici family began to emerge, and in particular the man who may be called the founder of the dynasty: Giovanni di Bicci.

Justus Utens, *Cafagiolo,* 1599, Florence, Pitti Palace, Storeroom

The Medici came from the Mugello Valley north of Florence, where they had their first properties. Cafaggiolo was acquired by Averardo de' Medici, grandfather of Cosimo the Elder.

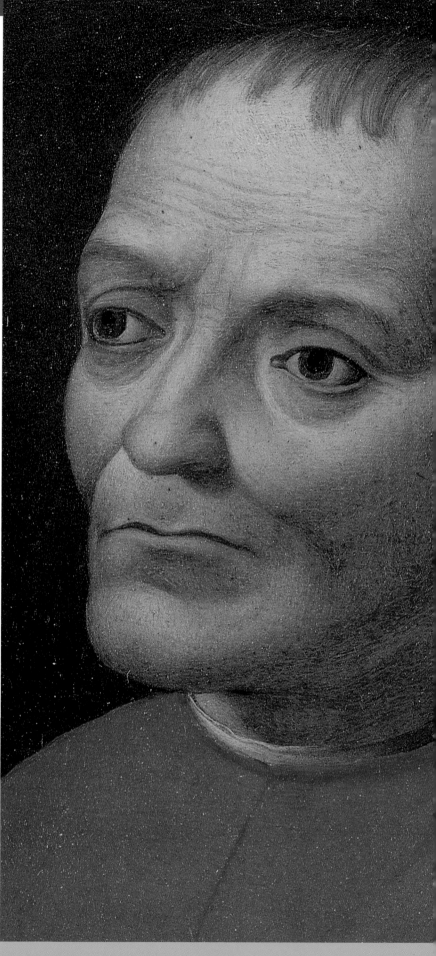

GIOVANNI DI BICCI

HE AND HIS FAMILY

CAME FROM THE

MUGELLO VALLEY.

EVEN THOUGH HE DID NOT

ASK FOR A POSITION OF

AUTHORITY IN THE

REPUBLIC,

IT WAS GIVEN TO HIM

AND HE ACCEPTED IT.

FLORENCE? 1360
FLORENCE 1429

AGNOLO BRONZINO WORKSHOP, *Portrait of Giovanni di Bicci*, 1555-1565, Florence, Uffizi

MICHELOZZO AND DONATELLO,
*Funeral Monument to the
Antipope John XXIII Coscia*,
1424-1427, Florence,
Battistero (Baptistery)

POLITICAL ROLE

In 1413, he managed to make an arrangement which any banker in the world at the time would have wanted to accomplish: he became Pope John XXIII's fiduciary agent, that is, his banker.

It is generally agreed that the Medici became the largest and most efficient economic and financial organisation of the time, and that Cosimo became the richest man in the world, precisely because of the family's involvement in the Papal Court's business affairs.

The family opened branches in Venice, Rome and Naples, continuing to finance Martin V and always maintaining due distance from all areas of political compromise. Nevertheless, partly in order to protect its many exiled friends, it skilfully introduced itself into Florentines public affairs.

As has already been mentioned, its interests were certainly not concentrated on political life. And yet, in 1418, it paid out the conspicuous sum of three hundred and eight thousand ducats in order to obtain Pope John XXIII's freedom.

When John XXIII, considered by the Church to be the antipope, died in 1419, the Medici erected a monument in his memory that can still be seen in the Baptistery, and on which they had placed an epigraph for which they were much criticised but which they refused to remove: *Quondam papa*.

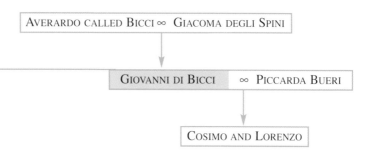

AVERARDO CALLED BICCI ∞ GIACOMA DEGLI SPINI

GIOVANNI DI BICCI ∞ PICCARDA BUERI

COSIMO AND LORENZO

In 1421, Cosimo was elected gonfalonier, thus clearly and decisively moving beyond the clamorous world of business. In 1426, this able, and very untypical, noble successfully instituted the cadaster, which was obviously of benefit to the Commune and to the detriment of the richest landowners, since it was a property tax. He was thus operating to his own disadvantage in the interests of the weakest.

In 1427, finally, when an attempt was made within the Seigneury to reduce the number of minor corporations and to remove the regulation prohibiting nobles from being elected, he obtained the people's approval to oppose the overbearing behaviour of the powerful nobles, relying only on his own authoritativeness and without imperial acts. He thus demonstrated his ability to impose himself politically.

This behaviour has a certain vein of demagoguery which the Medici were also to use in later years, as a way to obtain maximum popular consensus. This enabled them, by means of the shrewd use of carefully thought-out strategies, to acquire a degree of power that tended to become almost absolute.

Ospedale degli Innocenti
(Hospital of the Innocents), Florence

MASACCIO,
The Tribute,
1424-1427,
Florence, Santa Maria del Carmine,
Brancacci Chapel

View of the Sagrestia Vecchia
(Old Sacristy), Florence, San Lorenzo

ART AND CULTURE

There was an increase in the commissioning of works of art by private citizens during those years of major cultural ferment. In 1419, the Silk Guild promoted, with substantial financing by Francesco Datini, the construction of the Ospedale degli Innocenti (Hospital of the Innocents), carried out by Filippo Brunelleschi (who thus created the first Renaissance building); in 1425, the Calimala Guild commissioned Ghiberti to create the *Gate of Paradise* for the San Giovanni Baptistery; Felice Brancacci entrusted Masaccio and Masolino with the execution of a cycle of frescoes in the Carmine Church portraying *Scenes from the Life of Saint Peter* (1425-1428).

Giovanni di Bicci was also a prominent patron, commissioning Brunelleschi in 1419 with the reconstruction of the San Lorenzo Church, which would become the Medici church, almost a family temple. When Giovanni died in 1429, the church was nearly completed. He left his son Cosimo with the task of bringing it to completion.

And it will in fact be Cosimo who will determine the family's destiny and promote its interests and, governing in the background, those of the city itself.

LORENZO GHIBERTI,
Stories from the Life of Joseph,
1425-1452, Florence,
Museum of the Construction of the Cathedral

COSIMO THE ELDER

GIOVANNI DI BICCI'S HEIR, HE HAD A VERY STRONG CHARACTER, WHICH SOON BECAME APPARENT IN HIS WAY OF CONDUCTING THE FAMILY BUSINESS. BUT HE IS TO BE REMEMBERED MOST OF ALL FOR HIS INTELLECTUAL INTERESTS, PARTICULARLY IN THE AREA OF PHILOSOPHY.

FLORENCE 1389
FLORENCE 1464

AGNOLO BRONZINO WORKSHOP, *Portrait of Cosimo the Elder*, 1555-1565, Florence, Uffizi

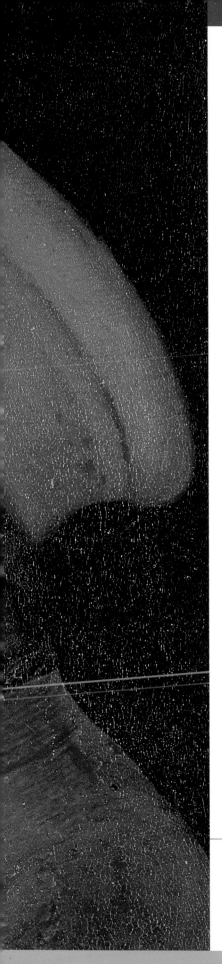

POLITICAL ROLE

He was known by all to be an upright man. The only fault attributed to him, and justly so, was his fathering of a bastard, Carlo, the result of his relationship with a Circassian slave but recognised and loved as the son he was.

Cosimo aligned himself with the people in two battles, and in doing so was aristocratically opposed by the Florentine nobles. Both events had disappointing results. The nobles conducted the war (1429-1439) against Lucca badly, while its defender, Rinaldo degli Albizzi, proved to be a skilful leader; Florence, intimidated by the fame of the Viscontis, fought a "useless war" in 1428, from which it emerged without glory even if not officially defeated. Cosimo succeeded in taking advantage of the resulting popular discontent and, placing himself at the head of the opposition, took the power into his own hands (even if in a republican regime,) without formally demolishing the city's institutions.

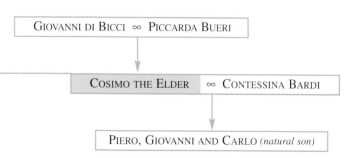

GIOVANNI DI BICCI ∞ PICCARDA BUERI

COSIMO THE ELDER ∞ CONTESSINA BARDI

PIERO, GIOVANNI AND CARLO *(natural son)*

Medici-Riccardi Palace, Florence

PAOLO UCCELLO,
Battle of San Romano,
variously dated circa 1435-1438
and circa 1456-1460, Florence, Uffizi

In 1434, the Medici family under Cosimo, who had just returned from exile, advanced imperiously towards the sovereignty of the city and of all of Tuscany, of which it would take control in the course of the century.

He did show a certain paternalistic trait, however, manifest with terse benevolence in the inscription on his tomb (he died in 1464), the synthesis of a life: *Pater Patriae* ("Father of the Country").

His artistic interests and the love with which he cultivated them help us to a better understanding of his character.

ART AND CULTURE

In 1456, he created a debating circle with Argiropulo, thus in fact founding the *Platonic Academy* with which Marsilio Ficino, who Cosimo always treated as a son, immediately associated himself. He gathered together an important collection of codices that became the nucleus of what would become the Medici-Laurentian Library. That this was a very serious and engaging undertaking is made clear by the fact that his "librarian" was the same scholar, Parentuccelli, who, when he later became Pope Nicolas V, created the Vatican Library.

Cosimo was also interested in painting, evidenced by the fact that he was frequently visited by painters such as Beato Angelico, whom he commissioned to do the main altarpiece for San Marco, and Paolo Uccello, who

BEATO ANGELICO,
"San Marco Altarpiece",
1438-1443, Florence,
San Marco Museum

DONATELLO AND WORKSHOP,
*Large lunette with bas-reliefs depicting
Saints Cosma and Damian*,
Florence, San Lorenzo, Sagrestia Vecchia

depicted for him the famous *Battle of St. Romano* in three episodes.

Because of his interest in the Camaldolite monk, Ambrogio Traversari, Cosimo, with his brother Lorenzo, commissioned Ghiberti to create a reliquary for the convent of Santa Maria degli Angeli (now in the Bargello Museum).

But his favorite sculptor was Donatello. He commissioned him to do the stucco decorations and the bronze doors in the Sagrestia Vecchia (Old Sacristy) of San Lorenzo. He had him create the statue of *David* and the *Judith and Holofernes* group. He entrusted Donatello with the realisation of the two bronze pulpits (which remained uncompleted) in San Lorenzo.

He showed even greater passion for architecture. Even though he could not but admire Brunelleschi (who, in 1436, completed the cupola of the Duomo begun by Arnolfo a century and a half earlier), he could not tolerate

DONATELLO AND WORKSHOP,
"Resurrection-Pulpit";
on the left detail of
the *"Passion-Pulpit"*
with the *Crucifixion* and the *Lamentation*,
1461-1465, Florence, San Lorenzo

FILIPPO BRUNELLESCHI,
Cupola of the Duomo

DONATELLO,
The Door of the Martyrs,
Florence, San Lorenzo,
Sagrestia Vecchia

the artist's difficult personality and was as little fond of his overly refined art. Brunelleschi, aware of his own worth, did not conceal his ambition of influencing present and future architects in direct competition with him, nor a certain intolerance towards those who commissioned his work. Thus Cosimo, having broken off relations with Brunelleschi, was obliged to choose another architect when he decided to build the Careggi and Cafaggiolo villas and the city palace on Via Larga. He picked Michelozzo di Bartolomeo. Michelozzo had complete responsibility for the Medici palace, for the Badia Fiesolana (Fiesolan Abbey), as well as for the Convent of San Marco, Santa Croce and the Annunziata Church.

The palace was begun in 1444, according to the formal criteria of rusticity already used in Palazzo Vecchio (the Old Palace). Brunelleschi's influence is clearly visible in the courtyard, where Michelozzo essentially reproduced the arcade in the Ospedale degli Innocenti, while the fact that the courtyard itself was inspired by the courtyard in the Palazzo Vecchio also emphasised, in the correspondence in the architecture, the close connection which by now united the family to the government of the city.

The impressiveness of the business conducted by Cosimo was of enormous advantage to him in politics. He alone, thanks to the bank's profits, was able to allow himself the luxury of hosting two emperors, Frederick II of Germany and John Paleologo of Byzantium.

In addition, availing himself of numerous international contacts, he managed to obtain the transfer of the Council from Ferrara, where it had been scheduled, to Florence, so that it seems fair if also malicious to describe him as the "puppeteer" of Florentine politics (Vespasiano da Bisticci).

This solemn event was a strong stimulus to all the artistic activities. Fra Angelico, Benozzo Gozzoli and Gentile da Fabriano painted figures in impressive processions, representing the events with the superb choreography that had been imposed on all public events, each one of which was staged to glorify the family.

The work done by Paolo Uccello was of even greater splendour. He created the fresco of the *Flood* in Santa Maria Novella. Since the Middle Ages, the ark had been considered the symbol of the Church. Boniface VIII had interpreted it as a symbol of the unification of the Roman Church with the Orthodox Church. Considering that the Council, the task of which was to discuss that very unification, had been transferred from Ferrara to Florence at Cosimo's express wish, and that it was held in the Santa Maria Novella convent, explains why it has been recently claimed that the myste-

DONATELLO,
David,
1440-1450,
Florence,
National Bargello
Museum

rious figure, turned towards the right, looking straight in front of him, is that of Cosimo himself, who wished thereby to emphasise the importance of his role within the Council, in order to increase the prestige of the Medici family. He died in Careggi, and the attribute-epitaph that we referred to above, *Pater Patriae*, was well earned.

PAOLO UCCELLO,
The Deluge and Recession of the Waters, Sacrifice of Noah and His Exposure,
circa 1446, Florence,
Santa Maria Novella Museum

On the left,
view of the Palazzo Vecchio courtyard, and,
on the right, of the Medici-Riccardi Palace
courtyard in Florence

PIERO THE GOUTY

HE SUCCEEDED HIS FATHER
COSIMO AT THE AGE OF 48.
PIERO HAD A GOOD
CHARACTER AND WAS
ACCEPTED BY EVERYONE.
HE TOLERATED HIS
FATHER'S PREFERENCE FOR
GIOVANNI, EVEN THOUGH
HE HIMSELF WAS ALSO A
CAPABLE AND VERY
TALENTED MAN.

FLORENCE 1416
FLORENCE 1469

BENOZZO GOZZOLI, *Piero the Gouty*, detail of *Procession of the Magi*, 1459, Florence, Medici-Riccardi Pala

AGNOLO BRONZINO WORKSHOP,
*Portrait of Giovanni,
son of Cosimo the Elder*,
1555-1565, Florence, Uffizi

*Giovanni (1421-1463),
intelligent, sensible,
and trained for leadership,
had married
Ginevra degli Albizzi, who
belonged to a family hostile
to the Medici.
He was supposed to succeed
his father Cosimo
as ruler of the city, but he
predeceased him,
dying in 1463.*

POLITICAL ROLE

It at first appeared that he was going to be unpopular. Ever the rigorous merchant, desirous of managing his finances well, he decided to compile an inventory of all his properties, thus alarming and upsetting his many debtors, who were not without influence. Since he was able to conduct himself adroitly and honestly, however, he won the citizens' esteem, and in 1461 they allowed him to become gonfalonier.

In 1466, a conspiracy was organised against him and, a year later, he had to face and defeat a move against him by Molinella exiles. In May of the same year, the Seigneury declared that, given the exceptional nature of the times, citizens qualified as the "Three Best" had to swear an oath of loyalty to the constitution, re-establishing the Guarantees that had lapsed in 1464, during the last months of Cosimo's rule. At this time, the opposition of Luca Pitti, Agnolo Acciaiuoli and Diotisalvi Neroni was defeated, and in August of 1466, a Seigneury favourable to Piero was elected.

Even though he was not the successor designated by Cosimo, who had preferred Giovanni, whom he considered to be more sound, Piero was a scholarly and trustworthy man, a good Latinist who had shown himself to be an excellent envoy for his father. Cosimo had entrusted him with delicate and complex missions to the rulers of other states. He had been in Venice to Francesco Foscari, to Milan to Francesco Sforza and to France to Louis XI.

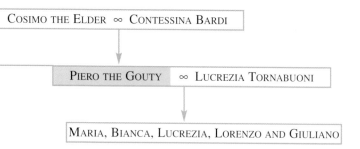

COSIMO THE ELDER ∞ CONTESSINA BARDI

PIERO THE GOUTY ∞ LUCREZIA TORNABUONI

MARIA, BIANCA, LUCREZIA, LORENZO AND GIULIANO

BENOZZO GOZZOLI,
Procession of the Magi,
1459, Florence,
Medici-Riccardi Palace

No diplomatic mission was ever carried out only as a matter of courtesy or for show, and the result, particularly in Paris, was so outstanding that the King of France had conferred upon him the privilege of placing the *fleur de lys* on one of the globes of the Medici coat of arms, as a sign of his admiration for the young noble.

ART AND CULTURE

His father Cosimo had ensured for him the advantages of a truly comprehensive education as a result of which, symbolic of his erudition, he had become a proficient Latinist. He was very interested in codices, of which he had many authentic samples. He also collected small rare objects like cameos and coins, an example of his tendency to order in the search for and conservation of objects, which he carried out in the manner of the most professional collector, a practice which he passed on to all the other members of his family.

In the figurative arts, while Cosimo loved to build, Piero decorated, gilded and embellished. Naturally, he had his favourite painters.

Among these was Domenico Veneziano who, in a letter written on April 1 1438, asked Piero to intercede with his father Cosimo so that Veneziano might be given the commission for a very important work, probably the main altarpiece for San Marco. He suggested that the other two painters under consideration (Fra Filippo Lippi and Beato Angelico (who later actually carried out the work) would not be able to undertake the task because they were involved in other projects.

It is very likely that Domenico, even though he was from Venice, was living in Florence in that period. Evidence of this is provided by the fact that he was responsible for the execution of the altarpiece in the Santa Lucia de' Magnoli Church for the Uzzano family (now at the Uffizi). In fact, it would appear that the luminous atmosphere created by the transparency of the

VERROCCHIO,
Sepulchral monument to Piero the Gouty and Giovanni de' Medici,
1472, Florence, San Lorenzo,
Sagrestia Vecchia

Santissima Annunziata Chapel, Florence,
Santissima Annunziata

work's delicate colours was taken into consideration when Leon Battista Alberti wrote his dictates in his *Treatise on Painting*, published in 1436. According to Alberti, light and colour were inextricably connected and hence the bright colours and luminosity of Domenico Veneziano's altarpiece are an obvious manifestation of the theories expressed in Alberti's treatise. Alberti shows himself to be in sympathy with the tendencies of the period, as demonstrated by his own assiduous frequenting of the world of Florentine painting and his assimilation of its point of view.

Benozzo Gozzoli also often benefited from Cosimo's commissions. Beato Angelico assisted him in the realisation of a work commissioned by Nicholas V, who recognised in Angelico a major exponent of *religious humanism*. Piero gave Benozzo, who had benefited from Nicholas' recognition of his work, responsibility for the decoration of the palace chapel, where he used delicate, transparent colours and soft strokes, according to the expressive modes dear to the commissioner.

Michelozzo di Bartolomeo received the commission for the small temple in Santissima Annunziata and for the crucifix chapel in San Miniato al Monte, but he had already done a great deal of work for the Medici, beginning work on the palace for them in 1444.

Luca della Robbia interested Piero because of the excellent quality of his technique and because of his skilful use of materials in a relatively unusual combination: marble and glazed terracotta.

In conclusion, it should be noted that Piero, who ruled officially for only five years, was initially undervalued, even if it should also be remembered that, as a diplomat in his own city, he was unable to avoid alienating the supporters and signers of the "Three Best" oath of loyalty. As long as he was alive, moreover, no one dared to oppose him openly and when he died, there was considerable uncertainty about what would be the result of one of his last decisions, that is, that his son Lorenzo, barely twenty-one years old, should take his place.

Crucifix Chapel,
1447-1452, Florence,
San Miniato al Monte

LORENZO THE MAGNIFICENT

THE ATTRIBUTE "MAGNIFICENT" WAS GIVEN TO HIM BY HIS CONTEMPORARIES. IN FACT, BECAUSE OF HIS DIPLOMATIC ADROITNESS, HE WAS ABLE TO MAKE FLORENCE PROSPER. HIS EXTRAORDINARY MERCANTILE POLICY MADE IT THE "NEW ATHENS".

FLORENCE 1449
FLORENCE 1492

AGNOLO BRONZINO WORKSHOP, *Portrait of Lorenzo the Magnificent*, 1555-1565, Florence, Uffizi

POLITICAL ROLE

When Piero died, his enemies were unable to bring down the Medici seigneury. The Medici had a large following of authoritative citizens in Florence, among whom Luca Pitti was prominent. In addition, Lorenzo, well aware of Pitti's vacuity and avarice, managed to neutralise him with substantial offers of money and honours, thus distancing him from the anti-Medici faction. And, since an attempt on Piero's life in 1466 had failed because of Lorenzo's incisive intervention, the seigneury showed no mercy in their condemnation of the conspiracy's instigators and organisers. Luca Pitti and Diotisalvi Neroni were sentenced to death, while Agnolo Acciaiuoli and Niccolò Soderini were sent into exile. In this way, the anti-Medici faction was dispersed and annihilated, for which the Pitti were held responsible because of their betrayal. Lorenzo declared, seeming to be alluding to the lives that had been saved: "Only he who is able to win is also able to pardon". Lorenzo was to be remembered throughout history for this unusually moderate point of view.

He was soon able to resolve the crisis caused by the transition of power, making modest adjustments to the communal institutions and thus assuring him control. As a means of consolidating and maintaining his power, he gave a few trusted allies the responsibility for preparing, each year, the list of citizens chosen for important offices. He was astute enough to leave the

PIERO THE GOUTY ∞ LUCREZIA TORNABUONI

LORENZO THE MAGNIFICENT ∞ CLARICE ORSINI

LUCREZIA, PIERO, MADDALENA, GIOVANNI *(later pope Leo X)*,
CONTESSINA E GIULIANO *(later Duke of Nemours)*

View of the first cloister with the Pazzi Chapel, Florence, Museum of the Construction of Santo Croce

The noble Pazzi family took part in the conspiracy staged in the Florentine cathedral on April 26 1478. Giuliano was felled by dagger blows; his brother Lorenzo the Magnificent took refuge in the Mass Sacristy.

political assemblies intact, transforming their role from one of deliberating to that of simply consulting. The Commune's most representative magistrates, that is, the Capitano del Popolo and the Podestà, became mere judges.

Until 1471, and in spite of considerable efforts on the part of the Florentine exiles, political equilibrium was maintained, with Florence and Naples allied against the power of Venice. After the death of Paul II, the newly-elected Pope, Sixtus IV (1471), wanted to create a new Pontifical State. Under the influence of his nephews Riario and Della Rovere, who shared his ambition in this regard, a papal alliance was made with Naples, and the overall political situation became dangerous.

Lorenzo's attempt to counterbalance this move by aligning himself with Venice, and thus making himself the promoter of an open League, failed. In Rome, in the meantime, Riario and the Florentines who were rivals of the Medici – including Francesco Salviati, Archbishop of Pisa, and the Florentine Pazzi family – organised a conspiracy against Lorenzo and his brother Giuliano. Although on the whole he was opposed to the conspiracy (historians are in disagreement about this opposition), he was unable to prevent it. Lorenzo and Giuliano were thus attacked during the celebration of Easter mass in Florence's Duomo (April 26 1478). Giuliano was killed; Lorenzo was only slightly wounded. The Florentine people were enraged by this event and their reaction had horrifying consequences, leading to three days of atrocities. A hundred or more well-known citizens were hung or massacred. Entire families, such as the Pazzi, were almost completely destroyed. The body of Archbishop Salviati dangled among the many other bodies hung from the windows of the Palazzo Vecchio. But the living and the death were hunted down. Those who had supposed that the Florentines would have preferred Pazzi to Medici rule were grossly mistaken, otherwise the populace would not have responded to Jacopo Pazzi's cry of "Liberty, liberty!" with "Bollocks, bollocks!", the battle cry typically used by Medici supporters.

When the Pope heard the news, he insistently demanded at least two immediate reparations: the return of the Cardinal Legate he had sent to Florence in an attempt to convince the city to obey – and which chronicles of the time described as returning to Rome more dead than alive – and exile for

View of the Mass Sacristy, Florence, Duomo

SANDRO BOTTICELLI,
Adoration of the Magi,
circa 1475, Florence, Uffizi

Many members of the Medici family are portrayed in this painting: the three Magi can be identified as Cosimo adoring the Child, along with his sons Piero and Giovanni; standing beside them, Lorenzo the Magnificent; opposite Lorenzo, on the extreme left, Giuliano; Agnolo Poliziano is leaning against Giuliano and Pico della Mirandola is standing beside Poliziano.

Lorenzo de' Medici. But Lorenzo, obdurate and convinced of popular favour and support, remained in Florence. Sixtus IV did not relinquish his thirst for revenge. He joined forces with King Ferrante of Naples and marched on Tuscany. In the summer of 1479, at Poggibonsi, the papal and Neapolitan forces routed the Florentines, occupied Certaldo and began the march on Florence. Lorenzo now demonstrated why he was called "Magnificent", since he decided to go to Naples to confront the ferocious monarch and to attempt to break the latter's alliance with the Pope. The Naples-Florence alliance was necessary – Lorenzo would argue – for the preservation of the independence of all of Italy. Lorenzo's audacious move was successful. Because of brilliant operations such as this one, which was an unexpected and resounding success, and because of the skill that Lorenzo continued to demonstrate in similar circumstances, he became known as the "needle of the scales" of Italian politics. He undoubtedly brought great good fortune to the peninsula.

Machiavelli identified as follows the only factor that prevented Lorenzo from guaranteeing the effective independence of the Italian States: "The ruin of Italy has been caused by none other than the fact of having depended for so many years on mercenary armies". That is, without a national army, the war was lost from the very beginning and not even a man like Lorenzo would have been able to win it.

ART AND CULTURE

The following critical definition of Lorenzo provided by historian Fred Bérence, while perhaps a bit extreme, is certainly worthy of note: "A man who misses nothing, to whom nothing is strange, nothing detestable, a man for whom nothing is either too noble or too base". The glorious days of Dante, Boccaccio and Petrarch were long past, but, under the auspices of the House of Medici, and particularly because of the example set by Lorenzo and his zeal, the worlds of science and of good taste were re-established.

Given a true scholar's education, Lorenzo's teachers included masters such as Becchi, Cristoforo Landino and, even Giovanni Argiropulo and Marsilio Ficino. The philosophical and literary encounters took place at such a level of fellowship that Ficino, in 1474, decided to enter a religious order only after having sought Lorenzo's advice. Ficino was still part of the Florentine Platonic Academy (which he had founded with his contemporaries, mentioned above), but he appeared to be worried that devoting so much of his time and energy to the study of a pagan author, no matter how great, was not completely compatible with his role as a Catholic priest.

The humanistic circle founded by Cosimo for the promotion of literature and culture, which by now had become famous throughout the world, attracted men such as Gemisto Pletone, who arrived in Florence among those who accompanied Emperor John Paleologo to the 1438 Council, and who remained in the city as the head of the Platonic Academy. And thus the school Cosimo had wanted to see established became institutionalised, given a Neo-Platonic stamp by the gifted Greek philosopher Pletone, who was joined in Florence by other Byzantine philosophers who had fled from Constantinople, which was occupied by the Turks in 1453. Among them were certainly Dimitrius Calcondila, Giovanni Andronico, Callisto, Costanzo and Giovanni Lascaris, while it seems that Giovanni Argiropulo, perhaps the greatest of them all, was already in Italy, in Padova, where he had given a number of conferences on Ariosto. It appears that a healthy competition developed in the Academy between the Greek philosophers and the Occidental intellectuals. Among the latter, philosophers such as Marsilio Ficino, Cristoforo Landino and Pico della Mirandola, and men of letters and artists such as Agnolo Poliziano, Luigi Pulci, Leon Battista Alberti and the young Michelangelo, stand out.

The Academy stimulated the setting up of public schools for the teaching of Greek where heated debates took place regarding the relationship between Christianity and pagan philosophy.

The revolutionary technical advances being made in printing were extremely useful for the distribution of many literary works. The Florentines and the Italians in particular made excellent use of the new means, which was also warmly embraced by many members of the Academy.

If it is true that many of the Academy's discussions revolved around the debate concerning the concrete possibility of making Christianity compatible with an indisputably pagan philosophy, it must also be noted that these discussions did not usually achieve any particular resolution of the issue,

SANDRO BOTTICELLI, *Primavera*, detail, 1482, Florence, Uffizi

Botticelli's famous painting is reflective of the cultured climate at Lorenzo the Magnificent's court. The painting belonged, along with Botticelli's other masterpiece, The Birth of Venus, *to Lorenzo di Pierfrancesco, the Magnificent's cousin.*

VERROCCHIO AND LEONARDO DA VINCI,
Baptism of Christ,
variously dated between 1473 and 1478,
Florence, Uffizi

ANTONIO DEL POLLAIOLO,
Hercules and Antaeus,
circa 1478, Florence,
National Bargello Museum

*This bronze, in which
Hercules is gripping
the giant Antaeus,
lifting him off the
ground in order to kill him,
was recorded in the Medici
Palace inventory after the
death of Lorenzo the
Magnificent.*

even though they did have profound influence on the way of thinking at the time. Even Clement VII, who was induced to intervene in the argument and who declared himself positively predisposed towards the consideration of the compatibility of the two philosophical doctrines, ran the risk of being considered a heretic. He was severely criticised for his point of view by Papal Court theologians, but, although he never denied his opinion, he did not make the error of proclaiming it publicly.

After Pletone, the following became the leaders of the academy: Marsilio Ficino, Poliziano, Landino and Pico della Mirandola.

Agnolo Poliziano (born in Montepulciano on July 14 1454), fled to Florence in 1473 after the murder of his father. In Florence, Lorenzo became his protector, offering Agnolo a place as a permanent guest in his house, thus making it possible for Agnolo to compete his studies. His studies must have already been well begun since he had been translating the *Iliad* into Latin hexameters since 1470, a translation which he dedicated to the Magnificent in the same year.

Lorenzo, himself a poet, became very fond of 15th-century poetry written in the vernacular. He was a capable author and wrote in various genres: from the *Rhymes* to short idyllic poems such as *La Nencia da Barberino* and *L'Ambra*, from lauds to carnival songs. An eclectic composer, he wrote musical verses that clearly owed a great deal to Petrarch but that were sufficiently autonomous as to be able to stand on their own.

Thus, he produced low-key texts such as the Ficino-inspired *Altercazione* as well as spiritual verses such as "O Dio, o sommo Bene, or come fai, / che te sol cerco e non ti truovo mai?" ("O God, who is so Good, how is it that / I search for You only and never find you?") Or the more successful and very well-known, "Quant'è bella giovinezza, / che si fugge tuttavia! / Chi vuol esser lieto, sia: / di doman non c'è certezza" ("How beautiful is youth / and yet how fleeting / If you want to be happy, then be happy now / for you know nothing of tomorrow").

Court celebrations, worldly sporting events such as jousts and hunts, and processions and dances exemplified the splendour of an era which will remain unique in history and which was also extremely rich from the philosophical and moral point of view. This was the reality in which the Magnificent lived and which he brought to life: he made Florence marvellous. San Bernardino of Siena was well justified in writing: "The country of Italy is the most intellectual part of the world; Tuscany is the most intellectual part of Italy; and Florence is the most intellectual city in Tuscany". The city's splendour did not include only magnificent works of art, but was reflected in the culture minds of the men of the Renaissance.

A man of such a complex cognitive personality, a man of such vast artistic interests, also obviously would want to commission works of art that would raise his city to even greater heights. In addition to confirming the commissions made by his predecessors, he commissioned works of his own, turning, for example, to Antonio and Piero del Pollaiolo, who had

already worked with Piero de' Medici. In fact, the Medici inventory of the time included, in addition to a painting of *St. John the Baptist* by Andrea del Castagno and to Pesellino's *Caged Lions*, three great paintings that Lorenzo was particularly keen on having done and which depicted *Hercules against Antaeus*, *Hercules against the Nemean Lion* and *Hercules against the Hydra*. The original works have disappeared; small copies, perhaps intended for the decoration of caskets or jewel boxes, have survived.

Andrea del Verrocchio was another of Lorenzo's superb collaborators. His workshop (where goldsmiths and sculptors worked as well as painters) included none other than Leonardo and Perugino. From among his paintings, *The Baptism of Christ* (1474-1475), done in collaboration with Leonardo, has survived. He created his *David* (today in the Bargello Museum) for the Careggi villa and, around 1480, the *Cupid with Dolphin*, kept in the Palazzo Vecchio, which is critically considered as being decisively innovative because of its original plasticity.

Giuliano da Sangallo (1445-1516) was the Magnificent's favourite architect. A follower of Brunelleschi, he began the construction in Prato, on his patron's orders, of the Santa Maria delle Carceri church, and surpassed his master in the difficult art of interpreting the aristocratic and Neo-Platonic ideals prevalent in the Medici circle. He was responsible for the Sagrestia di Santo Spirito and realised the Poggio a Caiano villa. Thus, Giuliano, in accordance with the tenets of Neo-Platonism, the predominating cultural philosophy in Florence, conceived of the idea of *perfect form* that exists before an architect creates his design.

He was also a military engineer and he formulated the project (1478) for the fortification of the city.

Yet another excellent architect among those dear to Lorenzo was Benedetto da Maiano (1442-1497), who constructed the Palazzo Strozzi according to criteria established by Michelozzo. He came up with a way to minimise the differences between the two ashlar floors in order to obtain an elegant, nuanced light and shade effect that gave surprisingly pleasing and new results. In the field of painting, the Magnificent's favourite was Filippino Lippi, whom he also recommended to other commissioners. As a result, Lippi became so famous that Vasari wrote that on the day of his death all the shops on Via dei Servi closed, as if a prince had died. Originally of the Botticelli school, he worked in Spoleto, in Florence in order to compete the Brancacci Chapel, and in Rome on Santa Maria sopra Minerva. A great painter, he worked for the Strozzi as well as for Lorenzo. In 1487, the Strozzi asked him to decorate the family chapel in the transept of Santa Maria Novella.

Lorenzo was a true prince. He actively participated in philosophy and in the world of letters; he discussed and wrote; he was a connoisseur of human virtues in the broad sense. He exploited all the opportunities which human nature gave him, in order to improve the quality of his own life and that of

VERROCCHIO,
David,
circa 1465, Florence,
National Bargello Museum

View of the Poggio a Caiano Villa

his fellow citizens. He was universally esteemed and admired. Gino Capponi summarises his value as follows: "Lorenzo was more audaciously resolute than Cosimo. His thinking, his artistic nature and his prince's soul expressed themselves over a much wider field of activity. He was the last embodiment of greatness in a splendid age that was coming to an end".

He not only enjoyed life with dignity but was also noble in his suffering. During the last years of his life, he forgot celebrations and parties, carnivals and dances and often fell into a state of anxiety in which the mystical predictions of Fra Girolamo Savonarola were likely not absent. Savonarola, with flaming Christian and anti-humanist fervour, insisted fanatically that power, which corrupted even through the exquisite works being created by the Renaissance, be replaced with the Kingdom of Christ.

And yet, when Lorenzo realised that he was about to die, he wanted Savonarola, who had been recommended by Pico, to attend to him. He begged Savonarola to give him absolution. His request was granted.

It is not difficult, finally, to agree with Angelo Fabroni, who wrote: "*vixit in laude et gloria, nec solum in civitate sua sed in tota Italia et universo fere orbe, cum summa aestimatione*" ("He was greatly esteemed, honoured and praised, not only in his own city but throughout Italy and throughout nearly all the world").

PIERO THE UNLUCKY

GOVERNED FROM 1492 TO 1494. HIS NICKNAME REFERS TO THE SERIES OF CATASTROPHIC ERRORS HE COMMITTED AND WHICH LED TO HIS OVERALL POLITICAL FAILURE. HE ALONE WAS IN FACT RESPONSIBLE FOR THIS FAILURE, BECAUSE OF HIS MEDIOCRITY AND IMMODESTY.

FLORENCE 1472?
GAETA 1503

AGNOLO BRONZINO WORKSHOP, *Portrait of Piero the Unlucky*, 1555-1565, Florence, Uffizi

POLITICAL ROLE

When Lorenzo died it seemed to be legitimate and natural that his twenty-year-old son Piero (or Pietro) should succeed him although he was not constitutionally a prince. Piero was brought into the Council of the Seventy and made a magistrate, in spite of his young age.

He was very highly cultured since he had received the customary, extremely thorough Medici education, and shared his father's interests for poetry and his love for the collecting of manuscripts. In addition, he had already tested himself in the political field, at the Sforza court and at the Roman Papal Court of Pope Innocent VIII.

He showed a certain degree of interest in the affairs of the family bank, which in that period was not prospering. In fact, it must be recognised that he inherited a heavily indebted banking operation, which made it impossible for him to assist "clients" economically with gifts and donations. Nevertheless, he enjoyed high prestige and success.

In politics, he behaved presumptuously. While Lorenzo had done everything in his power to maintain the Milan-Florence-Naples axis in balance, Piero gave clear preference to Naples. This alarmed Ludovico il Moro, who

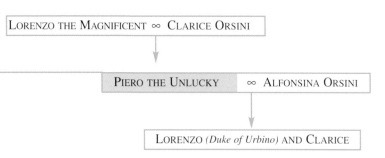

LORENZO THE MAGNIFICENT ∞ CLARICE ORSINI

PIERO THE UNLUCKY ∞ ALFONSINA ORSINI

LORENZO (*Duke of Urbino*) AND CLARICE

turned to Charles VIII of France for solidarity. The latter advanced him hereditary rights to the Kingdom of Naples and, profiting from the Milanese duke's need, took advantage of the opportunity in the autumn of 1494 to cross the Alps with the most impressive army ever to have done so. Ludovico gathered his own forces and together they began the march down through Italy. This invasion also lost Piero the sympathy of his citizens: his behavior had made enemies of both France and Florence. The two states' forces were so clearly unequal that there was no escape for the weaker side.

It is here that the most inconsistent sides and the most disturbing aspects of the character of Piero the Unlucky become evident. Mindful of the fine gesture made by his father in similar conditions, when, after the Pazzi plot, Cosimo went to beard the lion in his den, Piero wanted to meet Charles at the border.

Charles was not interested in conquering Florence, preferring to acquire strategic positions that would ensure him passage from north to south, and therefore asked for the fortresses of Sarzana, Ripafratta, Sarzanello and Pietrasanta, and the ports of Pisa and Livorno. Piero ought to have negotiated on the basis of this request, but, instead, accepted it, humiliating both himself and his city. He had submitted to unbearable conditions, acting on his own initiative without having consulted with or obtained the agreement of any of his fellow citizens.

When he returned to the Seigneury, he did so only to report on the outcome of the unfortunate mission, with the prudent foresight of having had himself escorted by armed soldiers.

Faced with such provocation, the citizens closed the doors of the Palace. Bells were rung calling the people to revolt and while the enraged crowd rushed to sack the Medici palace, Piero, with his brothers Giovanni

DONATELLO,
Judith,
Florence, Palazzo Vecchio

This group by Donatello was among the works confiscated from the Medici by the Seigneury after their expulsion. It was placed in front of the Palazzo Vecchio, where a copy of the original (inside the palace) can be seen today.

and Giuliano and their cousin Giulio, set out on foot towards Bologna.

It was November 9 1494, and while Piero was leaving Florence by means of the San Gallo Gate, heedless of the consequences of his act, the young Cardinal Giovanni, disguised as a Dominican monk, hid most of his valuable literary manuscripts in the San Marco convent. He also then escaped and joined Piero, who had reached Venice.

This was the second and most serious exile in the long period of Medici family rule. Piero died in a river accident during a military operation, in 1494, at the mouth of the Garigliano.

ART AND CULTURE

As has already been noted, Piero had the intellectual education and character typical of the Medici, as did his brother Giovanni, who became Pope Leo X.

But when Piero was exiled a veritable cultural calamity befell Florence. Tributes of four thousand and two thousand florins were imposed on Piero and Giovanni, respectively, and their flight left the inestimable family assets at the mercy of an angry crowd hungry for vengeance. The people, who had sacked the Medici palace from the roof to the cellar, including the treasures which had been accumulated there by Cosimo, Piero the Gouty and Lorenzo the Magnificent during fifty years of knowledgeable collecting, seemed intent on destroying everything in a savage outburst of destructive malice. Many of the furnishings and invaluable collections were stolen and dispersed and thus the entire society was deprived of artistic treasures that represented the summit of an intelligent and glorious process, now suddenly interrupted. Bernardo Rucellai, a scholarly chronicler, spares no ignoble detail in his description of the loss of the art treasures. He equally regrets the disappearance of precious manuscripts in all languages that had been jealously collected and informs us that Savonarola himself contributed to the saving of some of them, he perhaps regretting the bonfires made of so many wonderful treasures fanatically burned in the Palazzo della Signoria.

The long list of disappeared treasures is a measure of the offence done to culture. By the end of 1495, however, the Medici treasures were legally in Rome. Four valuable vases, on the other hand, remained in Florence where, in 1502, they were examined by Leonardo da Vinci at the request of Isabella d'Este. One of them, exquisite, was made of a single piece of crystal; a second was made of multicoloured jasper inlaid with pearls and rubies and mounted on a pedestal of gold; one was made of agate; and, finally, the fourth was of jasper, on a silver pedestal.

FRANCESCO GRANACCI, *The Entry of Charles VIII into Florence*, variously dated between 1518 and 1527, Florence, Uffizi, in

FLORENCE WITHOUT THE MEDICI (1494–1512)

A look must now be taken at the position that Florence came to assume in the European political context after the departure of the Medici and the simultaneous arrival of Charles VIII's army.

The first permanent army to move across Europe burst forcefully into Florence on November 17 1494 commanded by the King. Entering the city by the San Frediano Gate, mounted on horseback and with a triumphant demeanour, Charles arrived with provocative boastfulness. He was surrounded by ostentatious guardsmen and knights dressed in gold and brocade, Swiss and Gascon guards, the former bearing burnished weapons, halberds and decorations, while the latter were more moderately outfitted but were much more numerous. This was the first time that such an army had entered a free and independent, evolved and cultivated city, occupying it by force. In *The History of Florence*, Cerretani offers an emotional and disturbing description: twenty thousand men occupied the city. The display, however grandiose it may have been, was described by Guicciardini (who was twelve years old at the time) as frightening and terrifying. Charles, who had established himself in the Medici palace, wanted to challenge the Seigneury and invited it to sign a surrender immediately, threatening, otherwise, to sound the trumpets to bring the soldiers together and to complete the sack of Florence.

Faced with the famous contemptuous and threatening answer given by the noble Pier Capponi ("... and we will ring our bells"), Charles was intimidated and, in fear of being overwhelmed, preferred to postpone his demand. The treaty was signed much later but, all things considered, it was not much better than the scandalous treaty signed by Piero the Unlucky. In fact, the treaty stipulated that Pisa and the fortresses of Sarzana, Sarzanello, Ripafratta and Pietrasanta were to remain under Charles' control until he had taken Naples.

The Florentines also undertook to pay an indemnity of one hundred and

FLORENTINE PAINTER AT THE END OF THE 15TH CENTURY, *Martyrdom of Savonarola in Piazza della Signoria (Seigneury Square)*, circa 1498, Florence, San Marco Museum

twenty thousand ducats. Charles, satisfied, resumed his trek towards the south, terrifying Pope Alexander VI who, at the sight of an army more agitated than actually threatening, in any case retired to Castel Sant'Angelo and left the field open to Charles.

The King then continued on towards Naples, which he entered on February 22 1495. The conquest of the city was not an easy undertaking and because of the enormous expenses it entailed, Charles was obliged to leave part of his army behind and begin the return towards France faced with the declared hostility of Ferdinand of Aragon, the Pope, Emperor Maximilian, and even his former ally Lodovico Sforza. The battle took place on July 6 at Fornovo, on the banks of the Taro. It was the bloodiest battle fought in Italy in 200 years. Charles defended himself and even if he was not able to save his weapons and supplies, he in any case reached Asti on July 15 and remained there until October. The war, however negative it may have been with respect to the results achieved, did however serve as a test for so-called

FRA BARTOLOMEO,
Portrait of Girolamo Savonarola,
circa 1498-1499,
Florence, San Marco Museum

The Dominican priest from the convent of San Marco inflamed the Florentines with his apocalyptic sermons. After having been excommunicated by the Pope, he became an uncomfortable presence even to his own people and was hanged and burned along with two other priests.

San Marco Cloister,
Florence, San Marco Museum

"permanent" armies. In fact, with an army of this kind, made up of a force of nine thousand men, Charles held off forty thousand soldiers allied against him and occupying a superior position on surrounding mountains. But another aspect of this military event turned out to have a certain historical advantage: it revealed Italy, in all its complexity, to the nations of Europe.

Florence, unfortunately, without a leader or commander, found itself left outside the world of the other Italian states and while nearby states were engaged in struggles for supremacy in Europe, Florence continued to suffer from internal discord, the result of a debilitating fight between factions, none of which was able to prevail over the others.

It must also be taken into consideration that, in the meantime, major developments were taking place in the rest of the world: America had recently been discovered, Africa had been circumnavigated, commerce was being opened up in formerly unknown parts of the world or by means of new routes that led across the Atlantic towards the West Indies.

In Florence, the power vacuum made it possible for figures such as Savonarola to emerge. In response to the people's demand for more democracy, he formed the Grand Council, that is, a body composed of a thousand people of at least twenty-nine years of age, with a maximum period in office of six months. He encouraged the people to fight against luxury and licentiousness, organising the famous bonfire during the 1497 carnival, when worldly seductions and vanity were set on fire. As chronicles from the time describe, "[...] false hair, false beards, mask costumes, jars of lipstick, cards and dice, mirrors and perfumes, all manner of clothing and jewellery, books and drawings, busts and portraits of Florentine beauties [...]. As the flames rose up, the people burst out singing the *Te*

Deum, accompanied by the sound of trumpets and ringing bells".

Savonarola's irrepressible personality had also influenced some of the nobility: Baccio della Porta was so devoted to the priest that he became a Dominican monk in the San Marco convent, taking the name Fra Bartolomeo. Two members of the Della Robbia family became priests, Lorenzo di Credi entered the Santa Maria Novella convent, and Botticelli, from the time when he became Savonarola's disciple, created only works that were inspired by the latter's sermons. Cronaca wrote about him only, and Michelangelo was so deeply affected by him that he remembered the meanings and even the sound of Savonarola's sermons until he died. We have already mentioned Lorenzo the Magnificent's deathbed confession.

Savonarola, however, who had up until this point criticised only Florence and its corrupt habits, then took direct aim against Rome and the dissolute Popes, calling for reform. Rodrigo Borgia was Pope Alexander VI from 1492 to 1503. He was greedy, dissolute and perverse, grasping and immoral (he was the father of two children: Cesare, described by someone as "the virtue of the crime" and Lucrezia, who became even more infamous than her father). When he received news of the subversive priest's behaviour, he decided to intervene.

Savonarola was certainly not wrong to call for reform, especially for reform of many of the habits and practices of the time, even though objectively the historian Gregorovius wrote that because of Savonarola "everyone felt possessed by a fiendish element". Exasperated with his denunciations, the Pope saw to it that, on May 23 1498, Savonarola was hanged and burned, along with two other priests. His ashes were scattered in the Arno.

Before resorting to this extreme solution, Alexander VI had, in 1497, sent emissaries from the Seigneury to agree on terms for the arrest and convincing trial of the priest. The attempt was seen to be impossible from the very beginning and the trial became a tragic farce: in spite of repeated torture, of changing the Court (the Court of the Eight refused to take part), and of recourse to a special court, no one was able to wring a confession or an admission of heresy from Savonarola. The only answer, then, was to impose a false confession. But it was written in such improbable terms that its anti-historicity was clearly evident. Savonarola was killed and his murder gave many people the opportunity to become firmly convinced that the civility, authoritativeness and power of the Medici, of Lorenzo and of all the others, would never have allowed such a foul event to take place.

After the priest's death, the internecine conflicts between the Ottimati, the Bigi and the Frateschi resumed.

Fighting constantly amongst themselves, and even making arbitrary constitutional changes, they reduced the city to such a state of disorder as to marginalise it from the context that was making the civil development of the other states possible. Florence no longer had a functioning justice system, it abused its affairs to such a degree that the Grand Council refused even to authorise the money necessary for the state to pay its bills. Thus, aware that without a simulacrum of a leader or dictator they would not be able to progress, the Florentines decided to nominate a *gonfalonier for life*. They

chose Pier Soderini for this purpose, and he governed the city for a considerable period of time. Machiavelli assisted him with this delicate task, especially with regard to the management of diplomatic and military affairs. The two men were such good friends that because of the notoriety of their relationship, at the time of the attempted conspiracy by the Capponi and the Bossoli – in which Soderini was also involved – Machiavelli was suspected, imprisoned and tortured (February 1513). He was freed, along with Soderini, in March of the same year, as part of the universal exuberance surrounding the election to the pontificate of Cardinal Giovanni de' Medici: Leo X.

The Frateschi and the Bigi factions continued to fight each other and the White and Angry groups joined the fray. It is useful to recall at this point – even if only in passing – that while the palace on Via Larga was deserted, the "people's" branch of the Medici family was still living in Florence, the branch, that is, descended from Lorenzo, the brother of Cosimo the Elder.

In 1501, Alessandro Borgia gave Lucrezia as bride to Alfonso d'Este, the

RAPHAEL,
Portrait of Agnolo Doni
and *Portrait of Maddalena Doni*,
circa 1505-1506, Florence,
Palatine Gallery

*During his stay in Florence,
Raphael painted Maddalena Strozzi
and her husband, the wealthy
merchant Agnolo Doni, who had
also asked Michelangelo for a tondo
with the Holy Family, today in the
Uffizi.*

Duke of Ferrara, and continued to threaten the Republic of Florence through his son Cesare. In 1502, he informed the city that the government in office was not to his liking. He would certainly have intervened in his own particular fashion if Louis XII of France had not returned to Italy in the meantime (as the Florentines had hoped) to continue the war for Naples against Spain and if Alessandro had not died in 1503, either poisoned – as was at first believed – or because of natural causes. In December of the same year, the French where roundly defeated at Cerignola and immediately began to retreat in order to return home. As we have seen, one of the victims among their allies was Piero the Unlucky who, during the moving of a war carriage from a boat, was swept away and drowned in the waters of the Garigliano River.

Giovanni was left as head of the family (he would later become Pope Leo X). He was well liked and esteemed by many people who at first had been hostile to the Medici, and he enjoyed the friendship of Julius II. The latter, moreover, was fonder of war then he was of his institutional role, as a result of which, in 1509, he joined the Cambrai League against Venice, occupied Modena in 1510, and in 1511 seized Mirandola. In the same year, he again joined Spain and Venice in the anti-French Holy League. Having already defeated (1504) Cesare Borgia, he organised an expedition that forced Perugia and Bologna into submission (1506). He then attempted to involve Florence in his plans but Soderini unexpectedly resisted the temptation and remained neutral.

The French, involved in a new conflict in Ravenna, won the battle (1512) but, exhausted and depressed, did not feel able to continue the war and decided to return to France.

MICHELANGELO BUONARROTI,
David,
1501-1504,
Florence, Accademia Gallery

Julius II thus remained the real victor and as such demanded that Florence abandon its traditional friendship with France. During a meeting in Mantova, the League representatives decided on a definitive intervention in Tuscany in order to bring down Soderini. The Pope's envoy to this meeting was Cardinal Giovanni de' Medici, son of Lorenzo the Magnificent. The League army moved through Tuscany and conquered and sacked Prato, where it halted and where, it is said, not less than fifty thousand six hundred Pratesi were slaughtered on the streets of the city. The Florentines, meanwhile, were debating the conditions that had been imposed upon them: to join the League, to depose Soderini and to allow the descendants of Lorenzo the Magnificent to return to the city as private citizens. The crisis galvanised the existing factions and brought the Bigi, renamed Palleschi, into the open, as well as a large part of the opposition, encouraged by the Medici's request to reintegrate the Medici in their role as landlords in Via Larga. On August 31 1512, Soderini went into exile and on September 1 1512, Giuliano entered Florence.

There was no shortage of commissions during those turbulent years. In 1503, Pier Soderini asked Leonardo and Michelangelo each to create a fresco of a battle on the walls of the Hall of the Five Hundred in the Palazzo della Signoria (Seigneury Palace). Raphael stayed in Florence from 1504 to 1508, during which time Fra Bartolomeo and Andrea del Sarto dominated the artistic scene. Michelangelo's David, placed in front of the Palazzo della Signoria, became a symbol of civic virtue and a warning to the enemies of the Republic established after the removal of the Medici in 1494.

MICHELANGELO BUONARROTI,
Madonna and Child with young Saint John
("Pitti Tondo"),
1504-1505, Florence,
Bargello National Museum

PIETRO CANDIDO, *Portrait of Giuliano, Duke of Nemours*, 1586, Florence, Uffizi

THE RETURN OF THE MEDICI

If it is true that every people has the rulers that it deserves, Florence, the birthplace of Humanism and of the Renaissance man – that is, the prince, the condottiere, the cardinal, the courtier, the philosopher and the magician, the merchant and banker, and the artist – would not have been able to be governed for much longer by the ambiguous figures that had replaced the perhaps immoral but certainly brilliant members of the Medici family.

It was therefore decided that the Medici should return to take part in government, although they were not conceded absolute power. While Giuliano – who had returned to Florence more to reassume the privileges of his own family life than those of power – was prepared to play a politically distanced role, Giovanni and their cousin Giulio (the future Leo X and Clement VII, respectively) were unable to resist the pressure exerted by their own partisans for the elimination of the Grand Council that still represented the greatest degree of guarantee of republican freedoms. At the end of the reform, similar to that carried out by Lorenzo, and which began with this drastic amputation, the following elementary governmental structure was established: the Council of the Seventy, the Council of the One Hundred and the election of the Seigneuries by the Magistrates (who very soon were from the Medici camp).

The republic was in a state of decline because of the actions of Julius II. In addition, the Florentine people had lived through a long period of cultural and political eclipse, in the absence of leaders like Lorenzo, who only a few rash individuals went so far as to define as a tyrant. The population was tired of the arrogant behavior they had been obliged to tolerate during the Medici absence, during which time there was no economic or financial counterpart to the family whatsoever. The same applied to public order and safety.

It must be recognised that the two brothers, Giovanni and Giuliano, who had, like so many others of their fellow citizens, been obliged to submit to the destruction and sack of their home, did not seek revenge but rather, inspired by their father Lorenzo, practised the virtue of forgiveness. No capital execution, no expropriation, no victims. Normalisation was rapid and almost painless.

Giulio, their bastard cousin and future Pope Clement VII, had, on the other hand, a stronger character and a more audacious temperament. Afflicted with weak scruples, he had been Giovanni's constant companion, whom he had always thought of as a potential Pope. In fact, they had filled the empty hours of their exile by designing an elaborate project for the relaunching of the Medici in Florence, a project which they promptly began to realise. Giulio's efforts to have Giovanni named to the pontificate were crowned with success and other initiatives were undertaken to strengthen the Medici presence in the city. For the time being, it was a good thing that the government had been entrusted to Giuliano.

GIULIANO DUKE OF NEMOURS

THE LAST-BORN SON OF
LORENZO THE
MAGNIFICENT. FRANCIS I
OF FRANCE GAVE HIM THE
TITLE OF DUKE. HE
REIGNED FOR ONLY ONE
YEAR (1512-1513), BUT
HIS POLICIES
UNDOUBTEDLY HAD A
POSITIVE EFFECT ON THE
RE-ESTABLISHMENT OF
MEDICI POWER.

FLORENCE 1479
FLORENCE 1516

AGNOLO BRONZINO WORKSHOP, *Portrait of Giuliano, Duke of Nemours*, 1555-1565, Florence, Uffizi

MICHELANGELO BUONARROTI,
Tomb of Giuliano, Duke of Nemours,
Florence, Medici Chapels Museum

POLITICAL ROLE

As soon as he was installed in power, Giovanni and Giulio left for Rome, leaving him to rule Florence alone while they intrigued, successfully, for the conquest of the Papacy. He was considered a generous, charming and conciliatory man. This had also been the case when previously he had enjoyed success at the courts of Urbino and Mantova. It has even been claimed that he was one of the most attractive figures in the Italian Renaissance. He was not destined to rule for very long, but the single year of his reign was characterised by a general consensus, the result of a justified appreciation of his charming nature and of his widely recognised honesty. When Julius II died, Giulio de' Medici succeeded, as has been seen, in obtaining Giovanni's election to the pontifical throne. Once Rome had been conquered, it was necessary to strengthen Florence, where, in February of 1513, a new plot against the Medici had been discovered, organised by the young Pietro Paolo Boscoli and Agostino Capponi and a number of others, the most famous of which was Machiavelli. Leo X promoted Giuliano to Gonfaloniere to the papal army, obliging him to remain permanently in Rome and therefore leaving his role in Florence to pass into the hands of his cousin Lorenzo, the son of Piero the Unlucky, whose obedience to papal orders was well-known. Having thus achieved his objective of removing Giuliano from Florence, the Pope was not grudging of honours: he made him Prince of Parma, Piacenza and Modena, although he was unable to make him Duke of Urbino because of Giuliano's own direct opposition. Giuliano recognised Francesco della Rovere as the legitimate duke.

ART AND CULTURE

Giuliano had neither the time nor the means to commission any major works of art.

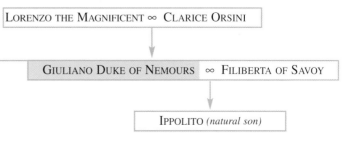

| LORENZO THE MAGNIFICENT ∞ CLARICE ORSINI |
| GIULIANO DUKE OF NEMOURS ∞ FILIBERTA OF SAVOY |
| IPPOLITO *(natural son)* |

LORENZO DUKE OF URBINO

OBEYING THE WISHES OF
LEO X, HE CONQUERED
URBINO AND TOOK THE
RELATED TITLE OF DUKE IN
1516. GIULIANO HAD
PREVIOUSLY REFUSED THE
SAME TITLE.

FLORENCE 1492
FLORENCE 1519

AGNOLO BRONZINO WORKSHOP, *Portrait of Lorenzo, Duke of Urbino*, 1555-1565, Florence, Uffizi

MICHELANGELO BUONARROTI,
*Tomb of Lorenzo,
Duke of Urbino,*
Florence, Medici Chapels
Museum

POLITICAL ROLE

He wanted to have more power at his disposal than what had been conferred upon him and demanded to be named overall Commander of the Florentines. Disappointed by the Pope's manifest intention to increase the involvement of the most important Florentine families, he did not include them, as he ought to have done, in the Council of the Seventy.

Shortly after his appearance on the political scene, he had already earned the contempt and hostility of everyone around him.

The Prince, as he considered himself, demanded to be able to make his own decisions, ignoring the Pope's wishes even though, when all was said and done, he had benefited from the latter's assistance. He was convinced that he was more powerful than the Pope was. Lorenzo died, in March 1519 – two years before Leo – and his wife, Madeleine de la Tour d'Auvergne, died around the same time, of puerperal fever. The death of this unpopular Duke was greeted by the Florentines with elation.

ART AND CULTURE

His premature death prevented him from any concrete manifestation of any interest he might have had in art and patronage.

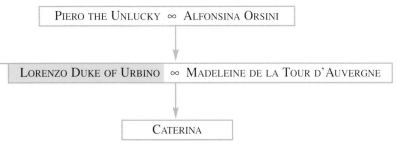

PIERO THE UNLUCKY ∞ ALFONSINA ORSINI

LORENZO DUKE OF URBINO ∞ MADELEINE DE LA TOUR D'AUVERGNE

CATERINA

GIOVANNI POPE LEO X

THE ELECTION OF LEO X
TO THE PONTIFICAL
THRONE IN 1513 WAS
JOYOUSLY RECEIVED IN
FLORENCE. A NEW
"GOLDEN AGE" WAS HOPED
FOR.

FLORENCE 1475
ROME 1521

AGNOLO BRONZINO WORKSHOP, *Portrait of Leo X*, 1555-1565, Florence, Uffizi

THE MEDICI AND THE PAPACY

POLITICAL ROLE

Lorenzo the Magnificent had understood that power in Italy could not be effectively held without a formidable presence in Rome, universal city and mother of the Church.

He therefore decided that his son Giovanni, at the age of eight years, after having been entrusted to tutors such as Pico della Mirandola, Marsilio Ficino and Agnolo Poliziano, should join the minor orders so as to be able to enter the court of Sixtus IV as apostolical prothonotary.

When Giovanni, having by then become a Cardinal, was named Pope on March 11 1513 by Cardinal Farnese, the people, mindful of the magnificence of the Medici court under Lorenzo, acclaimed him in the well-founded hope that the era of graces and favours would return. The young Pope did not disappoint their expectations. When the conspiracy in Florence, led by Paolo Boscoli, was discovered, he intervened with the families and arranged for the freeing of Machiavelli, Nicolò Valori and Giovanni Folchi, who had been involved (or suspected of so being) in the conspiracy. This both scholarly and hedonistic man was content with his investiture but, in fact, current opinion among scholars is that the growth of his own family was closer to his heart than the development of the Papal State.

Leo X is accused of many other things: of not having understood the importance of the Lutheran reform, of having granted the title of *Defender of the Faith* to Henry VIII of England (who would soon break with Rome), and above all, of not having undertaken a decisive diplomatic stance with Francis I and Charles V with respect to the struggle between them for supremacy over the Italian states.

LORENZO THE MAGNIFICENT ∞ CLARICE ORSINI

GIOVANNI *(Pope Leo x)*

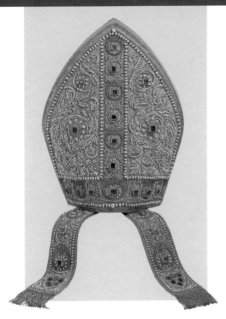

FLORENTINE MANUFACTURE,
Mitre,
first quarter of the 16th century, Florence,
Medici Chapels Museum

*Leo x gave this superb mitre to San Lorenzo,
the Medici's favourite basilica, a few steps
away from their palace.*

RAPHAEL,
Portrait of Cardinal Bibbiena,
circa 1516, Florence, Palatine Gallery

*The Cardinal and Raphael were close friends
and esteemed each other highly. Raphael was
given the task of decorating the Stufetta (small
stove) and the Loggetta (small loggia) in the
Cardinal's Vatican apartment, which he
painted with grotesque motifs, the result of his
studies of the frescoes in Nero's Domus Aurea
(Golden Residence), which had recently been
discovered.*

The Pope was also obliged to thwart a conspiracy against him in 1517, organised by Cardinal Petrucci in an elaborate and contorted way. It was Pandolfo Petrucci's plan to kill the Pope with the help of a surgeon, Battista Vercelli, who was to have done so by pretending to treat him for an anal fistula while in fact administering a poison through the fistula. Petrucci believed that his plan would succeed, but he was discovered and imprisoned in Castel Sant'Angelo along with the skilful surgeon and the other conspirators. Such was the life of the powerful and famous in those times.

The last aggressive event that took place during Leo x's Papacy was the return of the French army under the command of Francis I who, in the battle of Marignano in 1515, reconquered the Milanese.

The Pope was therefore able to pay greater attention to Florence and to what was taking place in the city. After 1519, there remained only illegitimate or unmarried members of the family that was so important to him. He identified Cardinal Giulio as the man who would be destined to take care of the family's political interests, thus preventing the transition from Lorenzo's rule from turning from restoration to usurpation. On the other hand, Lorenzo had been so disliked by his citizens that at his funeral in 1519 they, admiring and satisfied, followed Giulio's solemn steps in the lugubrious cortege dominated by the black of mourning, as he moved along in his splendid scarlet clothing, carrying a bouquet of roses of the same colour.

In the first phase of the war between Francis I and Charles v, the allied imperial and pontifical armies prevailed over the French. While Prospero Colonna chased Lautrech out of Lombardy, and Francesco Maria Sforza was being proclaimed Duke in Milan, the Church retook Parma and Piacenza. While on his way to celebrate the event, the Pope became ill and died, on the evening of December 1 1521.

ART AND CULTURE

An avid hunter and connoisseur, he enjoyed court life, which he filled with jesters, poets and ebullient guests. He was one of those who live life to the full.

He was a passionate collector, a prominent patron, and a friend of literary figures and brilliant artists. Pietro Bembo, an erudite poet and humanist from Venice, was among those he supported. In 1513, in Rome, Bembo published *De Imitatione*, in which he claimed the superiority of Ciceronian thinking with a dialectic skill that earned him the position of papal secretary. He and Leo x had Jacopo Sadoleto, a humanist and priest, write a poem in hexameters about the statue of *Laocoon* that has only recently been discovered.

But Cardinal Bibbiena (Bernardo Dovizi) was one of those who most benefited from his generosity. Bibbiena was the author of *The Fool*, a salacious comedy full of licentiousness, which the Pope evidently found very entertaining because the text was audacious and scintillating.

Lorenzo Pucci, datary during the time of Julius II, was benevolently named Cardinal.

And finally, Innocenzo Cybo, who was also promoted to Cardinal, perhaps only because he was the twenty-one year old son of one of Lorenzo's sisters, completed his entourage. Always aware of the influence that the

RAPHAEL,
Leo X with Cardinals Giulio de'
Medici and Luigi de' Rossi,
1518, Florence, Uffizi

Leo X's court of arms on the ceiling of the
Drawing Room in the Medici villa in Poggio
a Caiano

Wooden model for the façade designed by
Michelangelo for San Lorenzo, circa 1518,
Florence, Casa Buonarroti Museum

presence of cultured guests had had on his family in Florence, he invited Greek scholars to Rome; he acquired manuscripts for the Vatican Library and developed an intellectual salon.

He was fascinated by the ruins of ancient Rome and was saddened by their state of abandonment. His feelings in this regard were aggravated by Raphael, who wrote to him about the improper use that builders of the time were making of the ancient material. Leo X shared Raphael's disapproval and encouraged the resumption of excavations, entrusting the artist with the supervision of the project. He was very excited by the discovery of the *Bark* in front of Santa Maria in Domenica, of the enormous statue of the *Nile*, which he then had placed in the Belvedere Gardens, and of the colossal statue of *Tiberius*, also in the Belvedere Gardens.

A particular fault must be added to all these undoubted merits: his substantial contribution to the destruction of medieval Rome, which he encouraged in the continuous and somewhat ingenuous and inexpert intent of building a new Rome according to criteria acquired in his extensive studies. He had convinced himself that by rebuilding the city in the purest classical style, he would be helping it return to its ancient splendour.

The true value of this Pope was that he was an open and generous man of culture who gave concrete opportunities to artists during a particularly fertile period. His yearning for beauty led him to make audacious, perhaps too audacious, choices, even as far as his spending was concerned.

He allowed Raphael to continue to fresco the Heliodoros room and what was known as the Fire room, as well as to realise the cartoons for the tapestries destined for the Sistine Chapel, and to decorate the Vatican loggias. He also commissioned Raphael to paint his portrait, with two Cardinals, which remains one of the masterpieces of the genre.

He also named Raphael architect for the construction of Saint Peter's, which task he took over from Bramante.

It was the exuberance with which he expressed a parallel between the Arno and the Tiber, between Florence and Rome, in a sort of *ante litteram* twinning, that most revealed the Pope's tendency to think more about the growth of his family's image than about the development of Rome.

But the real architectural program was that conceived of for the façade of the family church, San Lorenzo. While the wooden façade of the Duomo only lasted for a short period of time, the new San Lorenzo façade would become the triumphant and permanent symbol of the Medici presence in Florence. The pontiff announced a competition, won by Michelangelo. The artist worked slowly on the project until 1519, when he abandoned it, perhaps partly because of the death of Lorenzo, Duke of Urbino, and the consideration that republican Florence might have reacted in a negative way to certain too peremptorily intrusive signs of Medici power. The Pope's intentions with respect to the San Lorenzo Church were not abandoned, however, and although the contract for the façade was cancelled, he, with his cousin Giulio, entrusted Michelangelo with the project for the Sagrestia Nuova (New Sacristy).

Finally, Leo X had the decoration of the central drawing room in the Poggio a Caiano villa completed, entrusting the task to Franciabigio, Andrea del Sarto and Pontormo.

GIULIO POPE CLEMENT VII

ELECTED POPE IN 1523, CLEMENT VII FOUND HIMSELF FACED WITH EXTREMELY SERIOUS SITUATIONS: THE PROTESTANT REFORM, THE SACK OF ROME, AND THE PROCLAMATION OF THE REPUBLIC IN FLORENCE.

FLORENCE 1478
ROME 1534

AGNOLO BRONZINO WORKSHOP, *Portrait of Clement VII*, 1555-1565, Florence, Uffizi

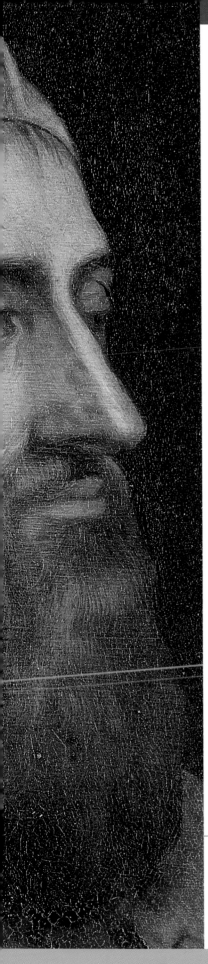

AGNOLO BRONZINO WORKSHOP,
Portrait of Ippolito,
1555-1565, Florence, Uffizi

POLITICAL ROLE

After the brief pontificate of Hadrian of Utrecht, Giulio de' Medici was elected Pope on the evening of November 18 1523. He was the second member of his family to take the pontifical throne and his election was greeted enthusiastically by all of Rome, which, remembering the Medici's famous munificence, was looking forward to the benefits of renewed splendour. The new Pope encountered great difficulty in living up to these expectations, but he showed himself to be an able navigator.

His first decision was to determine who would continue to rule Florence, now that he was obliged to remain in Rome. He decided that, since his own relatives were too young, Cardinal Passerini should administer the government even though it was formally still the responsibility of the Seigneury. This Passerini did for three years, as of May 1524.

He then sent Ippolito, the natural son of Giuliano, Duke of Nemours and grandson of Leo X, to Florence. Handsome and intelligent, he seemed to be the perfect choice for the city's future leader. He later also sent Passerini the young Alessandro, passing him off as Lorenzo's son when he was in fact his own natural son. With this expedient, which legitimised Alessandro's succession, he no longer maintained his original commitment to name Ippolito as leader, justifying his actions on the basis of blood ties. He thus preferred to opt for Alessandro the Moor, so-called because of his perennially tanned skin and thick mane of black hair.

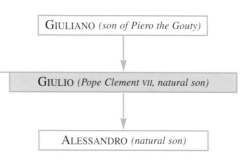

GIULIANO *(son of Piero the Gouty)*

GIULIO *(Pope Clement VII, natural son)*

ALESSANDRO *(natural son)*

BENEDETTO SQUILLI,
BASED ON A CARTOON
BY GIOVANNI STRADANO,
*Clement VII Receives a
Delegation of Florentines,*
1573, Florence,
Pitti Palace, Tapestry
Storerooms

The struggle between Francis I and Charles V made any hypothetical alliance with either of them very risky. The fortunes of these two combatants went up and down. In the last months of 1524 Francis I had triumphantly entered Milan, but then Charles V, in 1525, won the battle of Pavia, taking Francis prisoner and exiling him to Spain.

It seemed as though the Holy League, renewed in Cognac on May 22 1526, would have to move against Charles V and re-establish order in his ranks.

The King of England was the sponsor of the new League, while the Pope was its moral leader. The latter proposed to guarantee Francesco Sforza the Duchy of Milan, to free the sons of the King of France from captivity, and to chase the imperial soldiers from the peninsula. The situation seemed favourable to the Holy League: Genoa made Andrea Doria the head of the fleet, Giovanni de' Medici was leading the valiant troops of the Bande Nere, and Florence had a skilful diplomat in Francesco Guicciardini. It seemed as though, with this superb leadership, the League was invincible.

But all its hopes proved to be in vain. Charles V was saved by a throng of Landsknechts, thirteen thousand fanatical Lutherans who, having invaded the peninsula under the command of an adventurer, George Frundsberg, brought it to its knees. While the unstoppable invaders moved towards Rome, Clement VII, who had organised a weak defence under the leadership of Renzo de' Ceri (with four thousand men recruited at random), showed unexpected courage and instead of escaping to Civitavecchia, as he had been advised to do, moved through the streets of the city inciting the people to resist. Fruitlessly.

On May 6 1527, following the sack of Rome that produced rivers of blood and unheard-of atrocities, there were episodes of blind ferocity, as witnessed by this terrifying description, "[...] and the horrible stink of corpses, men and animals buried together; I saw corpses in the churches, gnawed on by dogs [...]. I now recognise God's justice, even if it has come late. All imaginable sins were being committed openly in Rome: sodomy, simony, idolatry, hypocrisy and deceit, and we may therefore believe that this has not happened by accident but that it is God's judgement".

Clement, in the meantime, had taken refuge in the Castel Sant'Angelo.

The imperial army had won and the Medici were therefore once again chased out of Florence.

Ippolito, Alessandro and Passerini headed towards yet another, melancholy, exile.

The city, in a last show of pride, and alarmed by the frequency of certain hostile events, considered it opportune to strengthen its natural defences by means of the construction of massive fortifications, in the execution of which Michelangelo was asked to apply his talents.

In the meantime, Clement VII, in the midst of so many misfortunes and disappointments, was nevertheless able to resume his vigilance over Florence, and was realistic enough to be able to manoeuvre the normalisation of relationships with the Emperor, meeting with him secretly in Barcelona in 1529. The pontiff came to an agreement with the Emperor and promised him a coronation, which took place the following year in Bologna. In return, he received the support of the imperial forces, which then besieged Florence, as well as the promise of a marriage between Marguerite, the natural

MICHELANGELO BUONARROTI,
Reading Room,
Florence, Medici-Laurentian Library

*In 1523, Pope Clement VII had
commissioned Michelangelo to design
the library where the Pope could keep
the valuable manuscripts that had
been collected since the time of
Cosimo the Elder.*

daughter of Charles V, and Alessandro de' Medici.

The siege began and the city's heroic defence proved to be of no avail. After strenuous resistance that lasted for ten months, weakened by plagues and privations, the Republic surrendered on August 12 1530. At this point, Clement VII, revealing the agreement concluded in Barcelona, made a very shrewd interpretation of it. Because of the understanding reached with the Emperor, a new formal and hereditary government of the Medici family had to be introduced with maximum consensus, the form of the government being preserved by means of the naming of an Authority that also included the choice of gonfalonier. The Grand Council was once again abolished. In 1531, Clement VII, acting skilfully through his diplomatic channels, also managed to have a special law passed that recognised the right of Alessandro, even though he was still very young, to participate in all aspects of government.

As we will see, he intervened many times in support of his restoration project, as in 1532, for example, when he forced the Authority to name twelve men (a kind of sub-authority) as "constituents" – including Francesco Guicciardini, Roberto Acciaiuoli and Francesco Vettori – thereby establishing the Medici as hereditary rulers in the Florentine constitution. Clement died in September of 1534 during the ceremony installing Alessandro in office.

ART AND CULTURE

He was a worldly man of good character who concerned himself above all with increasing the family's power, but also with the image of his posthumous glory, to which end he was an intelligent patron.

In Florence, he focused his attention on the San Lorenzo basilica. He had Michelangelo supervise the continuation of the work on the Sagrestia Nuova, on the reliquary Gallery in the church's counter-façade and on the large library annexed to the complex.

ALESSANDRO DUKE OF FLORENCE

ALESSANDRO TOOK OVER

THE GOVERNMENT,

RECEIVING THE TITLE OF

DUKE FROM EMPEROR

CHARLES V, AS WELL AS THE

HAND OF HIS DAUGHTER IN

MARRIAGE. HE TURNED OUT

TO BE A TYRANT, HOWEVER,

AND FELL VICTIM TO A

DEVIOUS CONSPIRACY.

FLORENCE 1511
FLORENCE 1537

AGNOLO BRONZINO WORKSHOP, *Portrait of Alessandro*, 1555-1565, Florence, Uffizi

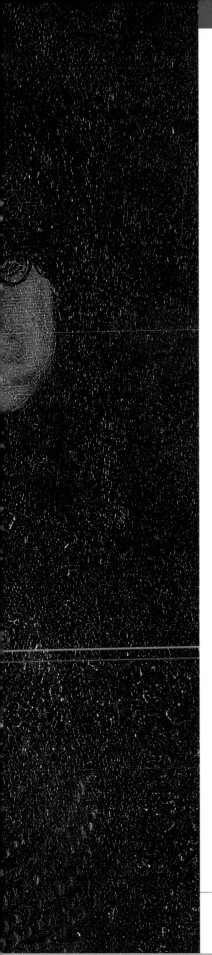

POLITICAL ROLE

By means of one of those arrangements which the powerful, thanks to the privilege of their position, are able to bring about, Charles V insisted that Florence remain a republic and that Alessandro be guaranteed control. Later on, this hypocrisy made it possible for the notion of direct inheritance to take hold, preparing the way for the Principality. This was an ignominious development for an ancient and glorious republic such as Florence, but times had changed.

A kind of "class war" was underway inside the city, inducing the aristocratic families to support the solution that was most socially and economically appropriate and functional for the interests of a principality.

In 1532, Clement VII guaranteed Alessandro by means of the new constitution, which included the sub-Authority and effectively abolished the Seigneury and the Gonfalonierato, replacing it with four Councillors to be elected every three months. These councillors constituted the "Supreme Magistracy" and, significantly, Alessandro was always their leader.

Alongside this magistracy were two Councils: the Council of the *Fortyeight*, responsible for foreign policy, and the Council of the *Two Hundred*, the tasks of which were of secondary importance – such as dealing with individual complaints of injustices, and taxes. These councils formally centralised most of the components of the main magistracies. As soon as this had been defined, Alessandro was able officially to give himself the title of "Duke of the Florentine Republic".

GIULIO *(Pope Clement VII)*

ALESSANDRO ∞ MARGUERITE OF AUSTRIA *(natural daughter of Charles V)*

Alessandro was thus the first Duke of the Medici, taking on this role when he was around twenty years old. Among the claims that Clement VII (Alessandro's real father; his mother, Simonetta, had been a servant in the Medici house in Rome) used to eliminate any competition from the perpetual rival Ippolito was that, since Ippolito was a member of the clergy, a Cardinal, he was excluded from aspiring to the title of Duke. It was in fact clear that neither would he have any heirs.

When Ippolito learned of Clement's manœuvrings, he became enraged, obtained the support of the Emperor, stirred up the people, and asked the Pope to return him to the laity. His efforts failed, as did his plots to eliminate Alessandro by means of a devious device placed under the latter's bed. His lover Giulia Gonzaga killed him in August 1535 in Itri, in circumstances that led the exiles to suspect that Alessandro had had him poisoned.

Alessandro was as frivolous, sensuous and brilliant as Ippolito, but certainly more cynical and cunning. He was described as being eccentric and informal, and showed some political skill, keeping the powerful on his side, often inviting them to the Medici Palace, while also listening to the complaints of the poor class with a good dose of demagoguery. He in any case could certainly never be defined as a gentleman. He was described, in fact, as a foolish and wicked young man, exemplifying the worst traits of human weakness. An example of the terror that he engendered in respectable people is given by the fact that no one dared to offend him or to correct him for fear of direct or indirect vengeance, such as the murder of their family members.

Charles V ought to have been put on his guard by Alessandro's character, but, instead, he gave him his daughter Marguerite's hand in marriage, according to what had been agreed

TITIAN,
Portrait of Ippolito,
1533, Florence, Palatine Gallery

Cardinal Ippolito (1511-1535) was more of a condottiere than a man of the church. Titian painted him in Bologna, dressed in the Hungarian style in memory of his undertakings in Vienna, which had been put under siege by the Turks.

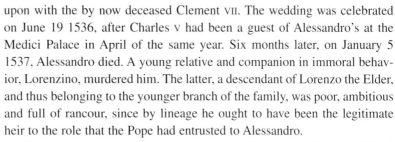

MICHELANGELO BUONARROTI,
Brutus,
1539-1540, Florence,
National Bargello Museum

Cardinal Ridolfi, who was an exponent of the anti-Medici faction, had Michelangelo sculpt this bust of Caesar's murderer in order to commemorate the assassination of Duke Alessandro by the latter's cousin Lorenzino.

upon with the by now deceased Clement VII. The wedding was celebrated on June 19 1536, after Charles V had been a guest of Alessandro's at the Medici Palace in April of the same year. Six months later, on January 5 1537, Alessandro died. A young relative and companion in immoral behavior, Lorenzino, murdered him. The latter, a descendant of Lorenzo the Elder, and thus belonging to the younger branch of the family, was poor, ambitious and full of rancour, since by lineage he ought to have been the legitimate heir to the role that the Pope had entrusted to Alessandro.

There are two versions of the way in which Alessandro was killed. According to the first version, Lorenzino, with the help of a hired assassin named Scoronconcolo, enticed Alessandro to his palace at night with the promise of introducing him to his beautiful sister Laudomia, the very young widow of Alemanno Salviati, and then killed him in a secluded part of the house. The second version has it that Alessandro was interested in Caterina, the beautiful and faithful wife of Leonardo Ginori, and Lorenzino, in order to draw Alessandro into the trap, promised him that he could meet the woman in the manner described above but killed him instead, with the help of the hired assassin. This took place in 1537.

Lorenzino also came to a bad end. Cosimo had immediately succeeded Alessandro as the head of the Florentine government and was afraid that his enemies would propose Lorenzino as the legitimate family heir. He pursued him in France, to which country Lorenzino had escaped, then in Turkey and finally in Venice, where he had taken refuge with his mother, Maria Soderini. There Cosimo had him killed by two hired assassins in a dark alley, on a night in 1548.

ART AND CULTURE

Alessandro commissioned no important works of art nor made any significant contribution to the valuable family collections. He was, however, sufficiently impudent as to commission two portraits of himself, by Pontormo and Vasari.

The latter explained that the iconography in his painting was meant to show, in the far background, that the nervous Florentine people had been reassured by the fortresses around the city, such as the Basso fortress, the work of Antonio Sangallo the Younger, which was also of considerable military value.

The fortress was actually a citadel, similar to those that existed in many other states, and was meant to represent the Prince's prudent defence against foreign aggression. In this case, however, it seemed more like a guarantee against possible local resistance.

Trollope wrote the following concerning the portraits of this misfortunate young man that he saw in the Florentine gallery: "[...] they show the baseness of the man, which derived from his physical characteristics. His small and contracted features, his low forehead and his degenerate appearance making him very different from the Medici line". Titian, on the other hand, who was the most famous portraitist of the time, had done a portrait of Ippolito that showed him to be handsome and seductive, like a true grandson of Lorenzo the Magnificent.

COSIMO I
GRAND DUKE

WITH COSIMO, ALL TRACES OF THE REPUBLICAN REGIME DISAPPEARED. FLORENCE BECAME THE CAPITAL OF A REGIONAL STATE AND THE ARTS WERE CALLED UPON TO CELEBRATE ITS MAGNIFICENCE.

FLORENCE 1519
FLORENCE 1574

AGNOLO BRONZINO WORKSHOP, *Portrait of Cosimo I*, 1555-1565, Florence, Uffizi

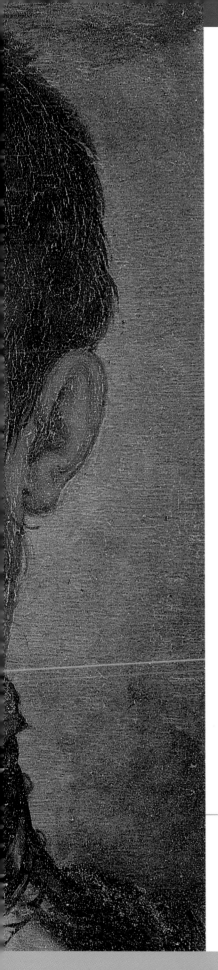

THE MEDICI GRAND DUCHY

POLITICAL ROLE

When Alessandro was assassinated, the news was kept secret until Cardinal Innocenzo Cybo – who was also a Medici through his mother, Maddalena, the sister of Leo X – as the representative of Charles V, decided to name as ruler the son of the condottiere Giovanni delle Bande Nere, Cosimo, who was eighteen years old at the time.

The Cardinal convinced the four principal senators, Guicciardini, Strozzi, Valori and Acciaiuoli, to accept his choice. They were relatively easily convinced because, being ambitious and convinced that Cosimo was easily manipulated, thoughtless and irresponsible, they thought that they would be able to control him easily. They soon learned that this was not to be the case.

In Montemurlo, near Prato, on August 1 1537, the exiles, including Filippo Strozzi and Baccio Valori, and with Piero Strozzi at the head of four thousand foot soldiers and three hundred knights, were beaten by the Florentine army, reinforced with Spanish troops and led by Alessandro Vitelli.

The Montemurlo victory revealed Cosimo's violent and revengeful nature. Having captured his adversaries' leaders, he had the Bargello,

GIOVANNI DELLE BANDE NERE ∞ MARIA SALVIATI

COSIMO I GRAND DUKE ∞ ELEANOR OF TOLEDO *(in 1539)*

∞ CAMILLA MARTELLI *(in 1571)*

With Eleanor: MARIA, FRANCESCO, ISABELLA, GIOVANNI, LUCREZIA, PEDRICCO, GARZIA, FERDINANDO AND PIETRO
With Camilla: VIRGINIA. *Natural son and daughter:* BIA AND GIOVANNI

AGNOLO BRONZINO WORKSHOP,
*Portrait of Giovanni
delle Bande Nere*,
1555-1565, Florence, Uffizi

AGNOLO BRONZINO,
*Portrait of Eleanor
of Toledo with Her Son Giovanni*,
circa 1545, Florence, Uffizi

GIOVAN BATTISTA FOGGINI WORKSHOP,
Bust of Cosimo I,
1723-1725, Florence,
Medici Treasures Museum

where the Council of Justice and the Rotating Judge were located, opened for them. It was rare that anyone, once inside the Bargello, came out of it alive. In fact, the numerous noble prisoners who ended up in these law courts after the defeat received no mercy from Cosimo even though they were often his own young friends. They were tortured, and put to death in groups. Those for whom there was no room in the crowded Bargello received the same treatment in the Fortress. Naturally, Baccio Valori was among the first victims, along with his son and Filippo Strozzi. In addition, Cosimo confiscated the Strozzi Palace and all the family's assets when Filippo was condemned.

At the time when these events were taking place, Cosimo was eighteen years old and was already mature enough to appreciate the good sense of announcing his submission to the Emperor. After having unsuccessfully requested the hand of the latter's daughter, Marguerite (Alessandro's widow), he did not lose heart but rather turned to the Viceroy of Naples, Peter of Toledo, and received permission to marry the latter's daughter Eleanor. The wedding took place in 1539. Eleanor was 16 years old, very rich, and although not beautiful was very charming.

After the marriage, Cosimo moved from Via Larga to the Palazzo della Signoria, where he was protected by two hundred Swiss and German guards housed underneath the Prior's Loggia, thereafter known as the Loggia d' Lanzi.

Cosimo, with his pragmatic nature, displayed extraordinary skill in realising the development of the Duchy.

He managed to almost double its territory and his foreign policy, even if conceived of according to a prevalently imperial point of view – during his first years, almost as a form of vas-

Portrait of Garzia,
1555-1565, Florence, Uffizi

Agnolo Bronzino Workshop,
Portrait of Ferdinando,
1555-1565, Florence, Uffizi

Giovanni Antonio de' Rossi,
Cameo of Cosimo I,
1557-1562, Florence,
Medici Treasures Museum

This large cameo, in imitation of ancient cameos, portrays the reigning family in their "official" mien.

View of the Eleanor Chapel, frescoed by Bronzino between 1540 and 1546, Palazzo Vecchio, Florence

salage – made it possible for him to use the Spanish power in Italy in order to expand his own borders. Although his every attempt to absorb Lucca failed, he was successful in conquering Siena (1555). After its forty thousand inhabitants had been reduced to no more than six thousand and its provisions were exhausted, Siena surrendered to the siege in the month of April, while its defender Pietro Strozzi retreated with his troops to Montalcino, leaving the commander Blaise di Montluc, Marshall of France, to sign the surrender.

Cosimo built up a war fleet, instituted the Military Order of Santo Stefano, and took interest in the territory's resources, exploiting the Pietrasanta silver mines and the Carrara marble caves. He obtained the concession for alum production in Piombino and gained the strategic positioning of a garrison in Portoferraio. In 1569, following the success of all these initiatives, Pius V gave Cosimo the title of Grand Duke of Tuscany.

Cosimo, however, had by then retired from public life, in 1564, naming his heir Francesco regent. This took place partly as a result of his having suffered a great loss two years previously. In 1562, during a tragic journey to Maremma, Cosimo had lost his wife and two children. Giovanni had developed a malignant fever in Rosignano, and died as a result of it a few days later. The same fate befell Garzia; his wife Eleanor died shortly thereafter, devastated by the death of her children and surely suffering from the same illness.

This woman had made a very significant contribution, including materially, to improving the Medici's lot. She had made her vast wealth available to her consort, as well as the powerful assistance of her father, who inserted pressure on the Pope to allow Cosimo autonomy and freedom of movement. She was a true, faithful, intelligent and devoted adviser to whom her husband listened all his life. The degree to which she was useful to Cosimo is demonstrated by his estrangement from the rest of the world when she, dying at the age of forty after twenty years of marriage, left him alone.

As we have seen, Cosimo, worn out, abdicated two years later. He did not neglect the duties of his rank, however, and after the funerals for his wife and children, he, in order to develop the family's contact with Rome, asked Pope Pius IV to name his son Ferdinando Cardinal. Pius IV agreed, even though it was a question of conferring the title on a boy fourteen years old.

View of the footbridge on
Via della Ninna, Florence

*The corridor that Vasari built in only five
months in order to unite Palazzo Vecchio
with the new ducal residence in the Pitti
Palace was conceived of as a secret and very
useful passageway that would provide a
rapid means of moving between the
administrative building and the private
residence.*

JUSTUS UTENS,
Belvedere with Pitti Palace,
1599, Florence, "Firenze com'era",
Topographical Museum

ART AND CULTURE

He was personally extremely interested in botany and created the Boboli Gardens and the Semplici Gardens, and instituted in Pisa what would become the Botanical Gardens, the most important garden of its kind in the world. Before going to live in the Palazzo della Signoria, in 1540, he assembled all the objects that had been removed from the Medici Palace in 1527.

He continued developing the collection of coins and medals begun by Lorenzo the Magnificent, and also had his ambassadors to other countries try, whenever possible, to buy Greek books and ancient sculptures. But the initiatives that he undertook and concluded, in which art, craftsmanship and economy were combined in the interests of the development of the state, were the most varied.

He entrusted Vasari with the most demanding and prestigious task: the transformation of the Palazzo della Signoria into a princely residence. In 1555, the architect took over the work begun by Del Tasso. He began by working on Leo X's Quarters, dedicating each room to an illustrious family figure according to a plan drawn up by Cosimo Bartoli. He then moved on to the realisation of the Elements Quarters, to making changes to the Eleanor Quarters and finally to work on the transformation of the Salone dei Cinquecento (Hall of the Five Hundred). In 1560, Vasari began the construction of the Uffizi and in 1565, during the time of the marriage of Francis I to Joanna of Austria, built a corridor to unite the Palazzo Vecchio to the Pitti Palace.

Pitti purchased the palace that came to be named after him from Bonaccorso. He had entrusted its expansion to Ammannati; Niccolò Tribolo created the garden.

Other initiatives worth remembering were: the decree that established the Florentine Academy in 1541, and the introduction to Florence, in 1546, of a group of weavers from Flanders, which Cosimo used to found a tapestry manufacture, led by Nicola Karcher and Jean Van der Roost. In the space of a few years, this manufacture was destined to become the pre-eminent tapestry production centre in Europe.

In 1547, he ordered work begun on the loggia on the new Market; in 1548, he had the Laurentian Library, designed by Michelangelo, opened to the public; in 1554 he had Cellini's *Perseus* placed in the Seigneury Loggia.

NICOLA KARCHER, BASED ON A
CARTOON BY AGNOLO BRONZINO,
The Dream of Mantiples,
border detail, 1549, Florence,
Palazzo Vecchio

Hall of the Five Hundred,
Palazzo Vecchio, Florence

In January of 1563, he established the Academy of Arts and Drawing, the first artistic academy in Europe. Made up of seventy painters, sculptors and architects, it was governed by six consuls. Vasari and Bronzini were members, along with sculptors such as Bandinelli, Romolo Ferrucci, Battista del Tasso, Sansovino, Cellini and Ammannati.

In 1566, he founded the Alterati Academy. He had the San Martino fortress built on the hills above San Piero in Sieve. He did not stop with this *extra moenia*, however, but had fortresses that were veritable monuments of military architecture built throughout Tuscany. San Martino, in particular, was begun by Cosimo and completed by his son Ferdinando I, based on a design by Buontalenti. A cannon designed by Michelangelo (now in the Bargello Museum and called the San Paolo cannon because the saint's head formed its breech) was a prestigious work of art created for this fortress.

Cosimo's last public commission was the pictorial cycle for the cupola of the Florentine Duomo that he entrusted to Vasari, but neither the Grand Duke nor the artist lived to see it completed, since both of them died in 1574.

Chimera,
end of the 5th century - beginning of
the 4th century B.C., Florence,
National Archaeological Museum

*Discovered near Arezzo in 1553, this
Etruscan sculpture was
acquired by Cosimo I.
Court intellectuals considered the three-
headed monster to be a symbol of the
Medici domination of the Grand Duchy.*

BENVENUTO CELLINI,
Bust of Cosimo I,
1545-1547, Florence,
National Bargello Museum

FRANCESCO I GRAND DUKE

HE ASSUMED THE REGENCY OF THE CITY IN 1564 AND RULED FROM 1574 TO 1587. SHY AND TACITURN, HE WAS NOT VERY SUITED TO THE MANAGEMENT OF PUBLIC AFFAIRS, AND DEDICATED HIMSELF TO THE SCIENCES, CONTRIBUTING TO THEIR DEVELOPMENT.

FLORENCE 1541
FLORENCE 1587

GIOVAN BATTISTA FOGGINI WORKSHOP, *Bust of Francesco I*, 1723-1725, Florence, Medici Treasures Museu

ALESSANDRO ALLORI,
Portrait of Joanna of Austria,
1568, Florence, Medici Treasures Museum

*In 1565, Francesco married Joanna of
Austria, sister of Emperor Maximilian II. The
wedding celebrations were elaborate and
ostentatious.*

POLITICAL ROLE

The events going on in Europe, with England and Spain involved in an exhausting and destructive naval war, France dealing with a ferocious internal conflict and the Low Countries torn apart by violent conflicts, ought to have made it possible for the Grand Duchy, which was not at the time part of the struggles, to have enjoyed a period of calm and of profitable development.

Assassins and conspiracies plagued Florence, however, and Francesco, in the first year of his reign, discovered the plans for a clumsy plot to take his life. This episode awakened in him the lowest of vengeful instincts. The Pucci family, Ridolfi Capponi and even Michelangelo, among others, were involved in the conspiracy. Those who did not manage to escape were slain. Those suspected of involvement were punished and stripped of their assets. Francesco thus also provoked the decline of many great Florentine families, and ended up being hated even more than his father.

Emperor Maximilian II, his brother-in-law, not taking into consideration a gesture already made by the Pope seven years before with respect to Cosimo, formerly conferred upon him the title of Grand Duke in 1576.

In foreign politics, he carried on the privileged relationships with Spain and with the Empire that had already been established by Cosimo, main-

```
┌──────────────────────────────────────┐
│ COSIMO I  ∞  ELEANOR OF TOLEDO       │
└──────────────────────────────────────┘
              │
              ▼
┌──────────────────────────────────────────────┐
│ FRANCESCO I  ∞  JOANNA OF AUSTRIA (in 1565)  │
└──────────────────────────────────────────────┘
                  ┌──────────────────────────────────────┐
                  │ ∞  BIANCA CAPPELLO (in 1579)         │
                  └──────────────────────────────────────┘
        │                                         │
        ▼                                         ▼
┌─────────────────────────────────────────────────┬──────────┐
│ ELEONORA, ROMOLA, ANNA, ISABELLA, MARIA AND     │ ANTONIO  │
│ FILIPPO                                          │          │
└─────────────────────────────────────────────────┴──────────┘
```

taining only formal relationships with France and the anti-Spanish Italian states. He thus continued to follow the diplomatic line created by his father.

But Francesco was not a statesman and, distant from direct involvement with the government, preferred to dedicate himself to alchemy and to science. He set himself up so as to be able to carry out pharmacological research, including research into poisons, by means of the use of insects and of thousands of scorpions, and even carried out experiments in perpetual motion.

There was very little that distracted him from his particular interests, not even two terrible family tragedies that befell him in 1576. His younger brother Pietro had married a fifteen-year-old cousin of their mother's, also named Eleanor. Pietro did not love her and steadily continued to indulge the vices that had always interested him, offending his wife with his indifference, and neglecting her to the point of driving her to betrayal with Bernardino Antinori. When Pietro learned of the adultery, he killed his wife in Cafaggiolo, stabbing her with a sword in a violent and self-serving version of a crime of honour.

Francesco's sister, Isabella, vivacious, intelligent and cultured, was courted by all those who appreciated her many talents. She spoke French, Spanish and Latin, she was a musician, a singer and a poetess. But these attractive qualities were of no interest at all to her husband, Paolo Giordano Orsini, Prince of Bracciano and a member of one of the most noble and influential Italian families. His interests led him in other directions.

But Paolo Giordano's handsome cousin, Troilo, dazzled and fascinated by Isabella's qualities, was both her tender lover and the reason for her condemnation, according to the customary motives of honour, sanctioned by her brother and by her husband. It would seem that there was an ambiguous agreement between the two, as a result of which the death sentence was issued with the understanding that the avenger should be her husband Paolo Giordano, in spite of the fact that Spanish tradition gave the role of vindicator to the brother of the faithless woman. Having agreed that Paolo Giordano should see to her death, he, with unusual courtesy, invited Isabella to accompany him to a villa belonging to Cerreto Guidi, where he

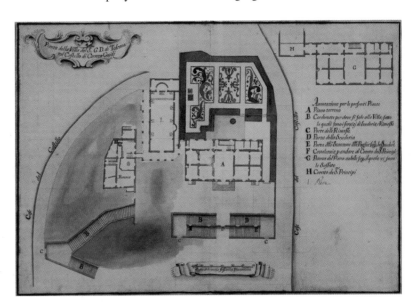

ALESSANDRO ALLORI,
Bianca Cappello,
Florence, Uffizi

Francesco I's Studiolo,
Palazzo Vecchio, Florence

then urged her to spend the night in Guidi's bed. This unusual request made Isabella very suspicious. Her fears proved to be well founded when, upon entering the bedchamber, she was strangled by the revenging hands of her husband.

Francesco was able to justify both crimes by classifying them as crimes of honour against the two adulteresses: Eleanor and Isabella.

Francesco's love life was almost equally obsessive. He became so infatuated with Bianca Cappello, an aristocratic Venetian woman of extraordinary beauty, that he ended up idolising her. She had run away from home with an impoverished young Florentine named Piero Buonaventura, for the killing of whom a reward of two thousands florins had been offered. Others maintain, on the other hand, that Piero, cynical and opportunistic, gained benefits from Francesco, who was weak and enamoured of the former's wife. These benefits led him to being introduced to the court. He was apparently also rewarded with a beautiful Palace in Via Maggio. The palace

BERNARDO BUONTALENTI (design),
JACQUES BYLIVELT (goldwork),
STEFANO CARONI (stonework),
Urn,
1583, Florence,
Medici Treasures Museum

had an apartment with an underground passageway by means of which he could reach the Pitti Palace. Piero, who had become arrogant and detestable, was killed, almost by chance, by a young man he had carelessly insulted near the Santa Trinita Gate.

Francesco even flaunted his lover Bianca Cappello in the presence of his wife, the Archduchess Joanna of Austria. Two months after her death in 1578, Francesco's new marriage was celebrated in great secret, and in October of the following year, the marriage was made public. Bianca became Grand Duchess of Tuscany, a position she held for nine years.

In October of 1587, Bianca and Francesco went together to the Poggio a Caiano villa. There the Grand Duke caught an influenza fever while hunting and insisted on treating himself with his own medicines, which were obviously ineffective if not outright dangerous, since they brought him close to death.

Bianca also came down with fever. When Francesco died, on 19 October, she, who had been suffering for the previous six days, just had time, because of the servants' agitation, to understand what had happened to her husband and then she too died, eleven hours later.

Ferdinando, in the meantime, had been sent to the villa to try to come to agreement with his brother concerning a number of controversial political issues. Since it was known that there was bad blood between the brothers and that Francesco's death would result in the throne being offered to Ferdinando, word spread that he had poisoned his brother and the latter's wife. Documentary evidence disproves this slander and confirms the illnesses that led to the natural deaths of the Grand Duke and the Grand Duchess.

ART AND CULTURE

Inclined, as has already been partly described, to a secluded life, Francesco, in order to be able to pursue his interests, commissioned the making of the *Studiolo*, a little room adjacent to the Hall of the Five Hundred in Palazzo Vecchio. It was a room of fine architecture and furnishings. Small cabinets, like little jewel boxes, filled rare and curious objects, were hidden behind splendid painted panels. Francesco asked many artists to participate in creating the design for the room, a design which focused on the relationship between the four elements (earth, water, air and fire). Among the artists were Vasari and Bronzino, Ammannati and Giambologna. Francesco had the latter, a Flemish sculptor, install the *Rape of the Sabines* in the Loggia de' Lanzi in 1583.

In his workshops – and especially in those in the Medici San Marco Lodge – he pursued his love of crystals, precious stones and ceramics, personally experimenting with their production, or commissioning precious objects from various court artists. The much-envied Oriental porcelain technique was emulated under his patronage.

Bernardo Buontalenti was his preferred artist, because of the man's extraordinary creativity and availability. Francesco turned to him for the execution of cups and vases of rock crystal and lapis lazuli but also for theatrical scenographies and celebrations with fireworks. The Grand Duke's

View of the Tribune as it is today, Florence, Uffizi

intellectual masterpiece was the Uffizi. The very term "gallery" derives from the use made of the corridors as ideal additional spaces for the exposition of the Medici collections. In the Tribune, designed by Buontalenti, a selection of masterpieces from the family treasure was collected. Still today, this octagonal room is much admired.

A great deal could be written about the villas that he purchased, restored or had constructed *ex novo*, such as the Magia di Quarrata villa, the Lappeggi villa and especially the Pratolino villa. The latter, built by Buontalenti, was surrounded by a park filled with grottoes, fountains and automatons, where Giambologna realised the colossal sculpture of the *Giant of the Apennines*.

Finally, he accepted with great pleasure Buontalenti's proposal to install and display Michelangelo's *Prisoners* in a grotto in the Boboli Gardens, in the midst of an exuberant display of rock fragments, shells and stalactites, creating a very impressive scenographic effect.

FERDINANDO I GRAND DUKE

IN 1563 (AT THE AGE OF 14 YEARS), HE WAS MADE A CARDINAL. IN 1587, ON THE DEATH OF HIS BROTHER, WHO LEFT NO HEIRS, HE RENOUNCED THE CARDINALATE AND BECAME GRAND DUKE.

FLORENCE 1549
FLORENCE 1609

GIOVAN BATTISTA FOGGINI WORKSHOP, *Bust of Ferdinando I*, 1723-1725, Florence, Medici Treasures Mus

GRANDDUCAL WORKSHOPS,
Medici-Lorraine Coat of Arms,
circa 1590, Florence, Opificio delle Pietre
Dure (Precious Stones Workshop) Museum

*The commission was perhaps carried out in
1589 on the occasion of Ferdinando's
wedding with Christine of Lorraine,
Caterina de' Medici's favourite
granddaughter. Caterina gave Christine all
her personal objects, which thus returned
from France to Florence.*

POLITICAL ROLE

During the years that Ferdinando spent at the Papal Court in Rome, he demonstrated that he had both excellent instincts for politics and diplomatic talent.

His service for the Church earned him much credit, as can be deduced from chronicles of the time, which indicate that he was being thought of as an almost certain future Pope.

Once he ascended to the throne as Grand Duke in 1587, he brought about a change in Florence's alliances, reducing its relationship with Spain and reinforcing that with France.

He had always remained in contact with Caterina de' Medici and married her granddaughter, Christine of Lorraine. The marriage was celebrated, according to what had been agreed, two years after the engagement, when internal conflicts and European wars underway during the period made it feasible.

Ferdinando's reign lasted for twenty-two years. The Grand Duke chose the motto *Majestate tantum*, "Only with dignity", which was a form of concrete reassurance of peace for the citizens, an expression of Ferdinando's commitment to eliminate violence in the exercise of power.

And so it was. He succeeded in re-establishing a climate of substantial equilibrium within the Duchy and in communicating a sense of a certain calmness to all those around him.

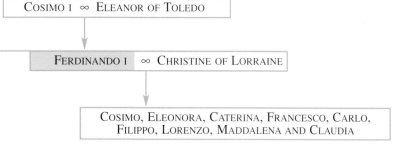

COSIMO I ∞ ELEANOR OF TOLEDO

FERDINANDO I ∞ CHRISTINE OF LORRAINE

COSIMO, ELEONORA, CATERINA, FRANCESCO, CARLO, FILIPPO, LORENZO, MADDALENA AND CLAUDIA

He restored the citizens' faith in civic institutions as well as a kind of pride of belonging that also derived from the many undertakings that he initiated, and in which he successfully involved the city's citizens.

He worked actively to consolidate the family's power by arranging successful marriages, beginning with his own, with the principal reigning European houses.

Always in search of opportunities for the family, in 1605 he successfully intrigued in order to bring about the election of Alessandro de' Medici to the pontifical throne. As Pope, Alessandro took the name of Leo XI. Although he was a distant relative, Ferdinando publicly showed his own gratification, with the skill of a gifted communicator, at the choice of a member of the family to the papal throne.

He was a man who was esteemed, and perhaps also even loved, by others. A significant summary of the popular consensus that he was able to gain is effectively expressed by the description which the Sienese dedicated to him and carved on the arch of the Camollia Gate in the direction of Florence: "Cor magis Saena tibi pandit". A heart turned in the right direction.

He died unexpectedly in 1609, at the height of his power, which he exercised with enterprising discretion and, finally, with a degree of balance not always shared by the other heads of the Medici family.

ART AND CULTURE

PIETRO AND FERDINANDO TACCA,
Ferdinando I,
1626-1642, Florence,
Medici Chapels Museum,
Cappella dei Principi (Princes' Chapel)

CESARE TARGONE,
BASED ON A MODEL BY GIAMBOLOGNA,
Fortification of the Belvedere in Florence,
1589, Florence,
Medici Treasures Museum

JUSTUS UTENS,
The Ambrogiana,
1599, Florence, "Firenze com'era"
Topographical Museum

*The Ambrogiana villa, the name of which
was taken from the Ambrogi, the first owners
of the estate, located in Montelupo
Fiorentino. It was constructed by Ferdinando
I who, having been named third Grand Duke,
had it built based on a design that was
perhaps by Buontalenti.*

Ferdinando certainly had extraordinarily lively cultural interests, of which it is important to furnish some details here. Even in his early days in Rome, he was a significant patron. He had collected ancient sculptures in his villa on Pincio and had sent others to his brother Francesco in Florence.

Once he assumed the throne, he dedicated himself to public commissions having especially to do with urban beautification. He turned to Giambologna for the equestrian monument to Cosimo I which, in the pedestal bas-reliefs, illustrates the salient facts of Cosimo's life, and which was set up in the Piazza della Signoria (Seigneury) in 1594. He also commissioned Giambologna to execute the equestrian monument to himself, completed by Pietro Tacca for Piazza Santissima Annunziata. Other statues in honour of Ferdinando were set up in other cities of the Grand Duchy: in Arezzo, in Pisa and in Livorno.

He proposed a law which prohibited the export of works of art without the previous consent of the Grand Duke and undertook to guarantee the conservation and expansion of the collections of rare and precious objects.

His principal credit, however, is the institutionalisation of work with precious stones by the foundation, in 1588, of the Works Gallery, later called the Opificio delle Pietre Dure (Precious Stones Workshop), which went on to produce work that became famous throughout Europe. The decoration of the Cappella dei Principi (Princes' Chapel) in San Lorenzo involved the manufacture for more than a century. This Chapel was a mausoleum in which the idea of death was exalted through the brilliant use of space. The spatial proportions express a form of human poetry tending more to a vision and a mirage of the future then to a metaphysics of the irreversible.

He had the Belvedere Fort, the Artiminio villa, and the Ambrogiana villa in Montelupo built, and restructured the Petraia villa.

His undertakings ranged from community initiatives, with the creation of the first convalescent home in Europe, to the financing of expeditions for the conquest of Brazil, in order to establish a foothold for Florence in the New World.

He interested himself in the development of the University of Pisa during the years just after Galileo's graduation, and appointed him to the chair of mathematics.

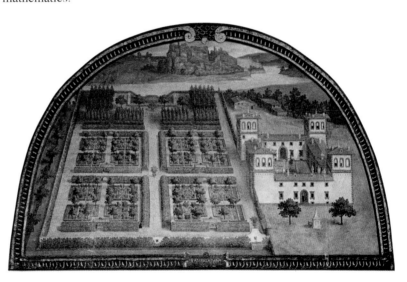

THE MEDICI IN LIVORNO

As a result of Ferdinando de' Medici's decisive and determined stimulus, Livorno became one of the most important Italian ports, equipped with piers, dikes and impressive docks. On his initiative, a draining canal was constructed between Livorno and Pisa and, in this way, it was almost as if a city arose as a function of its port and not vice versa. In 1590, in order to make this creation of his become an active and rich trading centre, he declared that it would offer asylum to anyone willing to start a business there or to help with the work, even if they were refugees, criminals or individuals on the run from other states. The historical conditions of the time resulted in the arrival en masse of entire ethnic or denominational groups, such as Jews who had escaped from Spain, Catholics from England and Protestants from France. Montesquieu was able to claim that Livorno was the Medici family's real masterpiece. Cosimo II was equally sensitive to the development of the city. He had Tacca add the statute of the Four Moors (which then became the name of the entire monument) to the monument which his father Ferdinando I had had erected to himself in 1595. Two fountains which were to have further embellished the work remained in Florence, in Piazza Santissima Annunziata, where they can still be seen today. In Livorno, he undertook the building of the pier that was named after him. It was realised in only seven years, and was based on a design by Dudley and Cantagallina, from an idea that had been proposed by Cogorano. Thanks to the Medici's intelligent investments, Livorno, which had approximately five hundred inhabitants in 1590, could boast of a population of fourteen thousand four hundred and thirteen in 1622.

"Habilità, privilegi et estensioni che il serenissimo Granduca di Toscana concede a quelli che verranno nel presente anno 1590 et 1591 ad habitare con le loro famiglie nella terra et porto di Livorno".
(Skills, privileges and expanses which His Serene Highness the Grand Duke of Tuscany concedes to those who, in the year 1590-1591, will come to live with their families in the land and port of Livorno).
Florence, October 8 1590.
In Florence, at Giorgio Marescotti's printworks.

National Central Library of Florence, Magl. 15.3. 144 11/c.45

GIUSEPPE MARIA TERRENI, *View of the Livorno Dock from the Windmill Rampart and the Porta Nuova Rampart*

Ferdinando I decided to commemorate the work he had done in Livorno with a monument. Giovanni Bandini portrayed him dressed as Grand Master of Santo Stefano. The execution of the project was entrusted to Pietro Tacca, who added the Four Moors, in memory of the Stefanian Navy's victories over the corsairs.

Bernardino Poccetti,
Map of Livorno and Allegory of its Prosperity,
after 1608, Florence,
Pitti Palace, Bona Room

CATERINA QUEEN OF FRANCE

FRANCE WAS TORN APART BY RELIGIOUS WARS AND THE "ITALIAN" WORKED PRUDENTLY AND WISELY IN ORDER TO MAINTAIN THE EQUILIBRIUM OF THE UNSTABLE MONARCHY.

FLORENCE 1519
BLOIS 1589

FRANÇOIS CLOUET, *Portrait of Caterina*, circa 1547, Florence, Palatine Gallery

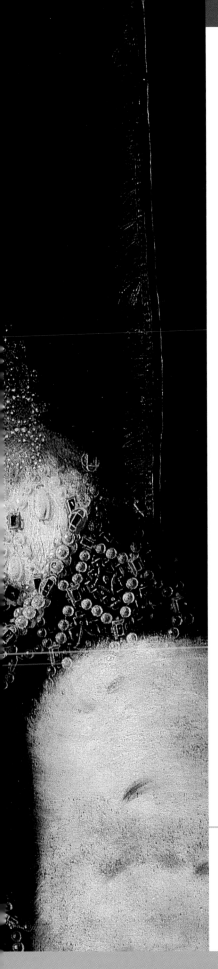

THE MEDICI QUEENS

FROM BIRTH TO MARRIAGE

(1519-1533)

She was born in Florence, on April 13 1519. Various nobles were present at her baptism, but not her parents. Lorenzo, Duke of Urbino and Madeleine de la Tour d'Auvergne were in such desperate straits that they would very soon both be dead. He of tuberculosis – although there are many who claim that it was actually a case of syphilis – and she of puerperal fever.

Orphaned, the baby was put in the care of her grandmother Alfonsina Orsini, in the ancestral palace in Rome, but unfortunately, she also died, on February 7 1520. In practice, then, Caterina was adopted by the wife of Filippo Strozzi, Clarice de' Medici, and was therefore moved to the Strozzi Palace. Clarice brought Caterina up as her daughter, along with her own children, and they remained very close for the rest of their lives. In 1525, at the age of six years, she returned to Florence, to the palace in Via Larga.

Clement VII claimed for her the assets that her mother had left in France, where he sent Roberto Acciaiuoli, a skilful diplomat and expert banker, to defend his granddaughter's interests. An agreement was made whereby the

LORENZO DUKE OF URBINO ∞ MADELEINE DE LA TOUR

CATERINA	∞ HENRY OF ORLEANS *(Henry II of France)*

FRANCIS *(Francis II of France)*, ELISABETH, CLAUDIA, CHARLES, HENRY, MARGARET AND FRANCIS *(Duke of Alençon)*

FRENCH MANUFACTURE (?),
Cameo with Caterina,
circa 1540, Florence,
Medici Treasures Museum

administration of the assets was taken away from the Duke of Albany, her uncle on her mother's side, who up until this time had made use of them without being controlled by the family. But threatening clouds were gathering on this young girl's horizon.

Dreadful years were in store for her. Between 1527 and 1530, she suffered the indirect consequences of the Sack of Rome, of Clement's defeat and of the extremely severe terms that were imposed on him, as a result of which the substance and very image of the Pope's power were weakened. Anti-Medici Florentines began to act with unrealistic but aggressive energy for the improbable return of the Republic. While being put under siege by the imperial army (1529-1530), they, lacking both judgement and any sense of honour, considered Caterina as a kind of valuable hostage protected only by the constant attention of her aunt, Clarice Strozzi, and therefore to all intents and purposes at their disposal.

Clarice, when she became aware of their adversaries' intentions, arranged for her niece to be taken to stay in the Santa Maria alle Murate convent of the Dominican nuns. The nuns were considered to be sufficiently neutral since they had been assisted by Countess Bardi, the wife of Cosimo the Elder, thus becoming tributaries of the Medici, although they later publicly sided with Savonarola, who was fiercely antagonistic to the family. It seemed as though this measure would sufficiently guarantee the young girl's protection, but such was not the case. She was in danger during every day of the siege, because of the hatred felt towards her by her besieged enemies, who believed that it was an advantage to them to have a legitimate heir of the Medici family so close to hand, one who could be used for possible exchange or blackmail.

One of the more vile proposals (apparently made by a certain Leonardo Bartolini) was to hang her from the walls that the besieging artillery where firing upon. Alternatively, it was suggested that her young body should be offered to the soldiers who made up the troops recruited by Florence.

When, in 1530, the city surrendered to the Pope, Caterina, who had moved to the San Gallo convent for a month, happily returned to the Murate until 1531, when Clement VII wanted her to return once again to Rome. She was twelve years old.

At the age of fourteen, the first suitors appeared. Among them were certainly the King of Scotland, the Duke of Mantova and the Duke of Milan. But, in 1532, Clement VII and Frances I had already agreed to give her as a wife to the King's second-born son, Henry of Orléans.

Caterina, who had been allowed to return to Florence, to her favourite nuns at Murate, finally left the city on September 2 1533 and travelled from La Spezia to the port of Marseilles, where a fleet of seventy ships was moored. The ship she sailed on had purple sails with gold brocade and a crimson satin canopy covered the deck. On October 28 1533, she married Henry in the Marseilles cathedral. Pope Clement VII officiated at the ceremony.

FRANÇOIS CLOUET,
Portrait of Henry II,
circa 1547, Florence, Palatine Gallery

FROM MARRIAGE
TO THE DEATH OF HENRY II

(1533-1559)

Caterina brought a dowry of one hundred thousand gold scudos. Fifty thousand were in cash and the rest was to be paid in instalments. Filippo Strozzi, an extremely rich banker and certainly from the financial point of view more reliable than a Pope, guaranteed the solvency of Clement VII, for whom he had raised the dowry. Strozzi later complained that his loan was never fully repaid, so that it was said that he in fact paid a part of Caterina's dowry.

Caterina's debut in France was certainly not particularly auspicious. She was unpopular because she was a foreigner and a descendant of merchants; she was suspected, because of the retinue of women and functionaries that she had brought with her from Florence, as if wanting to show off a kind of alternative court, replete with a personal perfumer, kitchen staff and maidservants entirely devoted to her alone. She manifested a resolute character and was in certain ways inflexible. In addition, she behaved like a classical Renaissance woman, actively concerned with problems of the spirit and religion, dialectically open and, as such, the object of obscure suspicions on the part of extremist Catholics. The latter had noticed, with some anxiety, that she spent considerable time with Francis I's sister (unfairly considered partial to Protestants), with whom she was often seen engaged in compelling conversations that certainly not all of those at court were able to follow. Many of them did not understand the open minds that the two women had in common and which rendered them somewhat inaccessible.

Caterina was also a woman singularly active in physical exercise. She taught the French women to ride sidesaddle and to practice the art of hunting, of which she herself was a highly skilled practitioner.

One of the unkind nicknames she was given was *Madame Serpent*, deriving from a malicious interpretation of her natural inclination to a courteous way of mediating among others. This nickname was used by the courtiers as part of their tactics against her.

This period of Caterina's life was marked by a particular tragedy. In 1536, three years after her marriage, Francis, the dauphin, died. This event suddenly placed her in the role of dauphine, since she had as yet not had any children of her own. Her barrenness seemed, at the time, to be an unforgivable fault.

VALERIO BELLI,
Coffer,
1532, Florence,
Medici Treasures Museum

Pope Clement VII gave this splendid chest to his granddaughter Caterina on the occasion of her marriage to Henry of Valois, heir to the throne of France, in 1532. It was inherited by Caterina's granddaughter, Christine of Lorraine, wife of Ferdinando I, who brought it back to Florence.

Finally, and not without the intervention of astrologers, diviners, philosophers and physicians, and after nine years of marriage, on February 10 1543, Caterina gave birth to her first child, Francis, who bore the same name as his grandfather. "The Sterile One", as she had been called, would go on to give birth to another nine children. Three died in early infancy; four males and three females survived. Of the males, three would ascend to the throne of France: Francis, Charles and Henry. Of the three women, Elizabeth married Philip II of Spain, Claudia the Duke of Lorraine and Margaret Henry of Navarre.

While Caterina was at first occupied with obtaining omens from the magicians' sorcery and witchcraft, and then dedicated to the demanding role of prolific mother, Diane of Poitiers had made her appearance in court. A powerful woman, gifted with indisputable beauty and convincing sensuality, she was the intriguing widow of the Seneschal of Normandy. She exercised irresistible influence on Henry, captivating him to the point of controlling him completely.

Caterina was able to face this difficult situation with such dignity and tact that she won the unconditioned solidarity of her father-in-law. Nevertheless, she endured ten extremely difficult years, partly because of Diane's hostile interference. Diane was treacherous and so protected by Henry that she could allow her self to call Caterina "the daughter of shopkeepers" with impunity or brazenly to take Caterina's place alongside the children's cradles while the "Italian" was giving birth to yet another child.

It becomes indeed difficult to define the true role and the essence of the character of the "Italian" from that time on. After the death of her father-in-law Francis I in 1547, she undertook to educate her children according to French custom and attempted to conform her own nature to that of her subjects, to the point where she won a legitimate place in their hearts. Such effort was made even more necessary because of the fact that her husband, once he

FRANÇOIS CLOUET,
*Portrait of Claude of Lorraine,
Duke of Guise*,
Florence, Palatine Gallery

*With France in upheaval because of the
religious wars, the Duke of Guise supported
the Catholics against the Huguenots.*

had ascended to the throne as Henry II at the age of twenty-eight years, continued to promote his favourite, Diane, in all the events of public life.

Caterina, an Italian woman in the Medici tradition and by now also in many ways a naturalised French woman, shared her family's taste for art and for building, an example of which is her having the Paris *Tuileries* designed and built, as well as the chateau at Chenonceau.

But her energies, which were neither few nor modest, were concentrated on the real and personal conquest of power after the death, in a fateful joust, of her husband Henry II, whose skull was fractured when an opponent's lance penetrated one of his eyes. Thus, in 1559, Caterina was left a widow.

FROM THE DEATH OF HENRY II TO THE DEATH OF CATERINA

(1559-1589)

Whether it pleased her subjects or not, Caterina was the most important figure in all of France for the next thirty years.

Three of her sons became king. The first, Francis II, reigned for sixteen months and died on December 5 1560. He was hated by the French because he was completely lacking in personality and determination, and had in fact left the governing of France to Francis, the Duke of Guise, and his brother, the Cardinal of Lorraine. During this period, Caterina remained excluded from power.

Her second-born son, Charles IX, succeeded his brother at the age of ten years, thus making it possible for Caterina, as regent, to assume the role of the wielder of power to which she inspired and which she retained for fourteen years, from 1560 to 1574.

Her third-born son, Henry III, died in 1589, at the age of twenty-three, after reigning for fifteen years.

Caterina was excluded from any interference in the reign of her son Francis II, while during the reign of Charles IX she was the true Queen. She continued to behave as the Queen when Henry III, whose advisor she had been since he was eight years old, came of age, preventing him from leading France into the disaster which her extravagant offspring had precipitated.

Since this now becomes more the history of France, which has little in common with that of Florence, we may summarise the rest of the events that transpired.

Caterina now had to face the religious wars. She was accused of having set off the bloody night of St. Bartholomew in 1572, in the organisation of which it seems that she was in any case directly involved because of her intransigent anti-Calvinism.

In 1586, she had to deal with her country's fourth civil war, after which, in addition to supervising the reign, she had to watch over her degenerate and mad son Henry III. During the celebrations around his coronation, Henry displayed himself in a very particular manner to the guests who had gathered in his honour. He was dressed as a woman, decorated with jewellery and heavily made-up. Caterina died on January 5 1589, six months before her son Henry III. Following the conspiracy against and the murder of the Duke of Guise – whom Henry had believed to be a competitor for the throne – he was assassinated in turn, by the League, in revenge for the killing of such a noble Catholic.

Maria Queen of France

The marriage desired by her uncle Ferdinando brought Maria to the throne of France. After the assassination of her husband, she became regent, but she was disliked and forced into exile.

Florence 1573
Cologne 1642

Frans Pourbus the Younger, *Portrait of Maria, Queen of France*, Florence, Pitti Palace, Royal Apartme

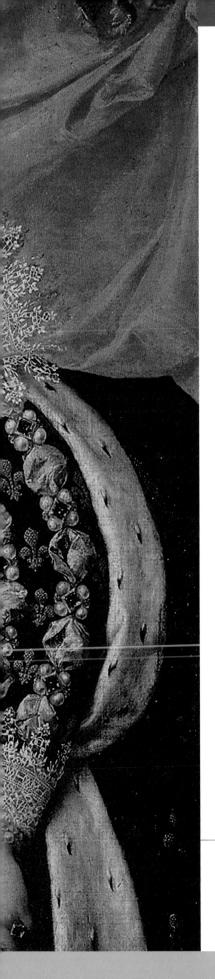

FROM BIRTH TO MARRIAGE
(1573-1600)

Maria, born in 1573, was six years old when her mother, Joanna of Austria, died and her place taken by the interloper Bianca Cappello, with whom the young child was obliged to live on her own. In 1582, her only brother, Filippo, died. Her sisters Romola and Isabella lived only briefly. Anna died in 1584 at the age of fifteen. Her only surviving sister, Eleanor, married Vincenzo Gonzaga, Duke of Mantova, in 1583.

In 1587, her father Francesco also died, and, only a few hours later, his great love, Bianca Cappello.

Maria, then, found herself in the custody of her uncle, Ferdinando I, of whom it seems she never grew fond. She always refused to be considered as his wife.

She spent her youth in the Pitti Palace, where her only friend was a woman who she would later take with her to France: Leonora Galigai.

Maria's marriage to Henry IV, after his divorce, with mutual consent, from Margaret of Valois, placed a Medici on the throne of France for the second time, but not without the good offices of Ferdinando, who sought to strengthen his family through these unions at the summit of European power.

FRANCESCO I ∞ JOANNA OF AUSTRIA

MARIA ∞ HENRY OF ORLEANS *(Henry IV of France)*

LOUIS, HENRIETTA MARIA, MARIE-CHRISTINE, ELISABETH, GASTON

The consequence of this marriage was that Maria became Queen immediately, at the moment in which, in October of 1600, she married Henry, while Caterina had had to wait for a very long time before being able to ascend directly to the throne.

The real reasons for these marriages were the interests of the parties involved: a question of high prestige for the Medici and of money for the French. The French, in fact, initially demanded that Maria bring a dowry of one million gold scudos with her. This amount was later reduced to six hundred thousand, happily accepted by the French representatives in the negotiations, since it was in any case a considerable sum.

Rubens (who later became the Queen's painter) portrayed the wedding ceremony in a great canvas: *The Delivery of the Ring* also called *The Proxy Marriage in Florence*, and masterfully reinterpreted in a splendid engraving by Jacques Callot, *Maria's Marriage*.

As always occurred in France on the occasion of extraordinary events, Paris, where the marriage took place by proxy, mobilised goldsmiths, interior decorators, organisers of performances, jugglers, clowns and lighting technicians, as well as, naturally, innkeepers, confectioners and vintners, all of whom produced a magnificent display for a superbly ostentatous ceremony. The official ceremony, when the marriage celebration effectively took place, was held at Lyon on December 17.

FROM MARRIAGE TO DEATH IN EXILE

(1600-1642)

PETER PAUL RUBENS,
Self-portrait,
1623-1625, Florence, Uffizi

Rubens had attended the marriage by proxy between Maria de' Medici and Henry IV of France in Florence on October 5 1600. The painter had the opportunity to meet the Queen again when she commissioned him to do a very large cycle of paintings depicting the significant episodes of her life. He finished this work between 1622 and 1625. The artist was her host in Cologne, where she died in exile.

The aversion of the French towards this woman who, for those times, was not particularly young, certainly not particularly physically attractive or exuberant, and who was apparently not very intelligent, began to manifest itself immediately.

She had a lifelong friendly relationship with an Italian couple that was anything but brilliant but that had undoubted influence over her: Leonora Galigai and Concino Concini, two intriguers and manipulators constantly in search of profit for themselves and of opportunities to placate their greed for money. Maria, as soon as she was able to do so, organised celebrations and ceremonies with her two questionable companions, and so doing turned everyone against her, including the extremely powerful Cardinal Richelieu.

Then, in 1610, Henry IV died suddenly. A fanatic stabbed him in his carriage while he was on his way to a celebration. Maria was regent until 1617, and her hunger for power and her fear of losing it drove her to depend on the loyal and evil Concini in order to prevent the interferences of court councillors. She compensated Concini extravagantly and even granted him the marquisate of Ancre. This time the reaction of her son, Louis XIII, was extreme.

He banished her to Blois, and from this time on her suffering began. In 1617, her friends the Concini were killed (not even Concini's wife was spared). Maria, after a number of attempts at reconciliation with her son, who recalled her in 1622 and then sent her away definitively in 1632, made a daring escape from the Blois chateau, to which she had again been sent, and immediately thereafter from France itself.

She went to Antwerp, where she lived in misery, subsisting on the little that her children sent her, in lodgings that the painter Rubens had put at her disposal. During the period of the exercise of her power, however limited, she had given important commissions to Rubens (for example, two paintings currently in the Uffizi Gallery: *Henry IV at the Battle of Ivry* and *Triumphal Entry of Henry IV into Paris*). Rubens was honoured to be her host even if she was by now in absolute and utter decline.

She died in Cologne, in total misery, in 1642.

GASPARD DUCHANGE (engraving),
JEAN MARC NATTIER (design),
The Queen Lands at the Port of Marseilles,
1710, Pitti Palace, Florence

The queen left Livorno on October 15 1600 and landed at Marseilles. This engraving, which depicts her arrival, is based, along with five others, on a cycle of paintings (now at the Louvre) by Rubens which Maria de' Medici had done to decorate the new Luxembourg Palace .

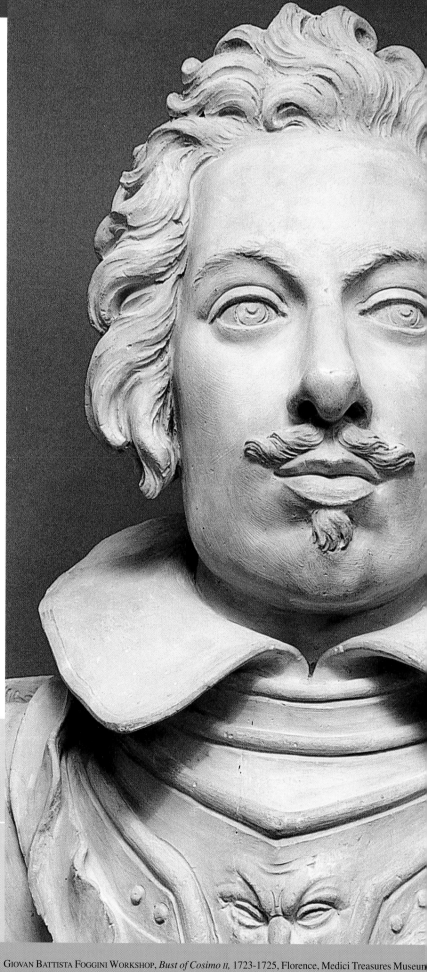

COSIMO II GRAND DUKE

HE HAD A NATURAL
GOODNESS OF HEART AND
WAS EXTREMELY WELL-
MANNERED, MAKING HIM
LIKEABLE AND WELL-
THOUGHT OF BY ALL. HE
SUFFERED FROM ILL HEALTH
AND WAS NOT ABLE TO PUT
THESE ADMIRABLE GIFTS TO
USE IN GOVERNMENT.

FLORENCE 1590
FLORENCE 1621

GIOVAN BATTISTA FOGGINI WORKSHOP, *Bust of Cosimo II*, 1723-1725, Florence, Medici Treasures Museum

THE LAST GRAND DUKES

POLITICAL ROLE

When he ascended to the throne, he rekindled the old family sympathies for Spain, manifesting, on the other hand, a definite antipathy for France. The good offices of the Duke of Lorraine were necessary for the normalisation of relationships, which appeared somewhat problematic.

In foreign policy, he undertook no other particular initiatives. He was the representative of a state that was in any case by now on the margins of the major international disputes and conflicts that were occurring at the highest levels, foremost among which was the Thirty Years War. His conduct is characterised by a few significant facts.

The first is his closing of the banking activity that had always been part of the tradition and means of support of the Medici family.

The second consisted of his favouring the return of Galileo, to whom he also gave a villa in Arcetri. He appointed him to the chair of advanced mathematics in Florence.

He devoted much of his attention to the navy. He succeeded in having warships built, with the help of Dudley, one of the many refugees to Livorno. He used the navy, manned and sailed by the Knights of Santo Stefano, to fight victoriously against the Druses and the Turks.

His nature, promising and gentle, was marked by illness to such an

FERDINANDO I ∞ CHRISTINE OF LORRAINE

COSIMO II ∞ MARY MAGDALENE OF AUSTRIA

MARIA CRISTINA, FERDINANDO, GIOVAN CARLO, MARGHERITA, MATTIAS, FRANCESCO, ANNA AND LEOPOLDO

PIETRO TACCA,
Cosimo II,
1626-1631, Florence,
Medici Chapels Museum,
Cappella dei Principi
(Princes' Chapel)

CRISTOFANO ALLORI,
*Portrait of
Mary Magdalene of Austria,*
before 1621,
Florence, Palatine Gallery

extent that he neglected his political responsibilities and the family's banking affairs which, as we have seen, he had voluntarily renounced.

He died on February 28 1621.

ART AND CULTURE

Cosimo II was only nineteen years old when he ascended to the throne and married Mary Magdalene of Austria but his reign, however brief, was very important for art and culture.

As of 1618, he gave Giulio Parigi the task of expanding the Pitti Palace, while the Grand Duchess entrusted him with rebuilding the Poggio Imperiale villa, which was pompously done over in honour of her Hapsburg origins.

A passionate collector, Cosimo II introduced genres of painting to Florence that had been neglected until that time. He invited Jaques Callot and Filippo Napolitano to the city and named Justus Sustermans

FLORENTINE MANUFACTURE,
Dog,
17th century, Florence,
Medici Treasures Museum

*The Grand Duchess
loved to surround
herself with dogs at
her Poggio Imperiale
residence. This small
ivory was inspired
by one of her dogs.*

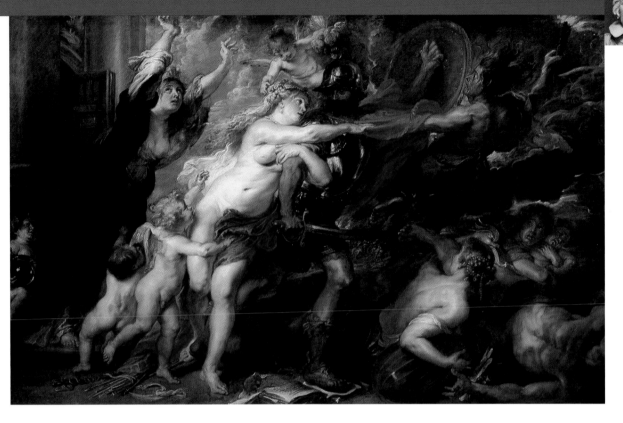

PETER PAUL RUBENS,
The Consequences of War,
1637-1638, Florence,
Palatine Gallery

When the artist sent the painting to Sustermans (who was also Flemish but who had by then become Florentine by adoption and the Medici portraitist), he illustrated the allegorical scene in reference to the 30 Years War that was devastating their country.

court painter (Sustermans had been the Medici portraitist since 1620).

Finally, he had the work on the Cappella dei Principi in San Lorenzo continued, and carried on with the construction of the port of Livorno, in order to promote the development of the city.

GRANDDUCAL WORKSHOPS,
Ex-voto of Cosimo II,
1617-1624, Florence,
Medici Treasures Museum

The ex-voto was to have been mounted on a frontal intended for the altar in San Carlo Borromeo in Milan. It never arrived in Milan, because of the death of the Grand Duke, shown here in the act of asking for better health, against a background with a partial view of Florence.

FERDINANDO II GRAND DUKE

THE FIFTY YEARS OF THE
REIGN OF THIS MILD AND
WEAK INDIVIDUAL COULD
HAVE BEEN THE
OPPORTUNITY FOR A
RENEWAL OF THE MEDICI
FAMILY WHICH, HOWEVER,
CONTINUED TO SLIDE
DOWN THE SLOPE
OF ITS DECLINE.

FLORENCE 1610
PISA 1670

GIOVAN BATTISTA FOGGINI WORKSHOP, *Portrait of Ferdinando II*, 1723-1725, Florence, Medici Treasures M

JUSTUS SUSTERMANS,
Portrait of Mattias de' Medici,
circa 1660, Florence,
Palatine Gallery

*The youngest son of Cosimo II, Mattias
(1613-1667), was sent to take up a military
career, in which he distinguished himself on
numerous occasions. He was nevertheless an
avid collector, shown by the fact, for
example, that while fighting valorously in
Coburg in 1632, he obtained thirty exquisite
ivory vases, now kept in the Medici Treasures
Museum.*

POLITICAL ROLE

Cosimo II, aware that his health was precarious, declared in his will that on his death the two Grand Duchesses, Christine of Lorraine and Mary Magdalene of Austria, that is, the mother and grandmother of the underage heir Ferdinando, should assume the regency together. He arranged for a series of codicils that should have protected the wealth and security of the state, as he was aware that the two women were, in reality, potential squanderers. Notoriously devoted to magnificence, both of them obsessed with luxury and ostentation and in competition with each other, they also had in common a costly bigotry which induced them to dedicate excessive attention to convents and monasteries, which undoubtedly enjoyed unexpected benefits and advantages. Word spread of such munificence and religious institutions began to increase significantly in number.

In short, the eight years of their regency were a veritable disaster.

Cosimo's recommendations were disregarded and a vast heritage, that Cosimo had also intended to be a form of insurance for the people in case of calamity, was dissipated.

Florentine commerce was experiencing a crisis because of tough competition in foreign wool and silk markets. Then, from 1632 to 1633, the city was devastated by another epidemic of plagues, just at the time when the

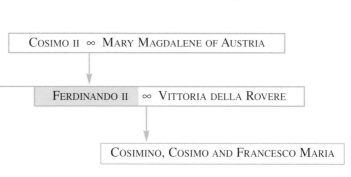

| COSIMO II ∞ MARY MAGDALENE OF AUSTRIA |
| FERDINANDO II ∞ VITTORIA DELLA ROVERE |
| COSIMINO, COSIMO AND FRANCESCO MARIA |

AUGUSTA WORKSHOPS,
Cabinet from Germany,
1619-1625, Florence,
Medici Treasures Museum

*Ferdinando received this
extraordinary ebony cabinet set
with precious stones as a gift from
his uncle Leopold v, the Archduke of
Austria, during his journey to
Innsbruck in 1628.*

government was obliged to face a financial crisis caused by an excess of expenses relative to earnings. The state coffers were empty.

Even though Ferdinando was still both too young and too inexperienced, it was decided to give him a wife. In 1623 therefore, on the return of his widowed aunt Claudia, along with her daughter Vittoria della Rovere, who was barely one year old, Christine and Mary Magdalene organised the engagement of the two cousins, with the intention of uniting the Duchy of Urbino and the Grand Duchy of Tuscany. The territorial union, however, did not take place. When the eighty-two year old Duke Francesco Maria II della Rovere died, Pope Urban VIII denied the only heir his rights to properties and holdings, recognising only his rights to personal goods.

It was thought suitable that Ferdinando should gain the experience he would need in order to develop the necessary confidence for appropriate exercise of power and he was therefore sent to Rome in 1627 to frequent noblemen and the Papal Court. He was however, discouraged by the unpleasant welcome given to him by the Barberini and decided to leave. He moved to Vienna and stayed with his maternal uncle Ferdinando II, but did not seem particularly stimulated by his court experience there. In 1628, at the age of 18 years, he returned voluntarily to Florence to take up his role as ruler.

His was certainly not an authoritarian approach but he was influential. He succeeded especially in organising economic and sanitary assistance for the population, which had been scourged by the plagues. He distributed money to the poor and to the corporations. The court, hoping to avoid infection, had isolated itself in Fort Belvedere, but Ferdinando saw to the creation of a proper Health Office, asking both the clergy and convents to participate materially in taking care of the ill. This was not a particularly well-thought of move in some quarters, and he was censured by the Pope, who rebuked him for having imposed laws which were actually in strict accordance with justice and equality. The pontiff was irritated by the fact that a certain kind of obedience had been imposed upon the clergy, particularly since it had been done by someone not authorised to do so, even if the objective was exclusively one of helping the Florentine community

Ferdinando was considerably morally affected by this move, given that he was still under the influence of his bigoted mother, a determining influence that continued until her death in 1631.

Ferdinando's long reign, begun under the worst auspices and with delay in the effective exercise of his rights as ruler, turned out to be more successful than had been foreseen.

Historians agree that he was an able, good, generous and cultivated man, gifted with a fine sense of justice. His contemporaries' opinion of him was similar. When he died, in 1670, he was consigned to history as a ruler equipped with the best human qualities but limited by his weakness, which reduced Florence politically to a city substantially without influence. The city was economically

View of the Giovanni da San
Giovanni Room, Medici Treasures
Museum, Florence

GIOVAN BATTISTA FOGGINI,
Cardinal Leopoldo,
1697, Florence, Uffizi

*The son of Cosimo II
and Mary Magdalene of Austria,
Cardinal Leopoldo (1617-1675) was an
extremely cultured man, an enthusiastic
and intelligent collector of works of art.
A fine connoisseur, he is credited with,
among other things, the establishment of
the beginnings of what is now the Uffizi
Drawings and Prints Studio, as well as
with assembling a collection of self-
portraits.*

poor even if rich in art, literature and science, a wealth that still today has
enormous value in the context of human culture. The Tuscan court of this
period was described in these terms: "one of the most splendid in Italy,
because of its art masterpieces, and where the rooms shine with the luxury
of the refined nobility [...] because of the sumptuousness of the balls, the
banquets, and the theatrical performances, and especially because of the
people who flock to it from all other countries. Not to mention the servants,
the black pages and luggage bearers, the horsemen and the carriers".

ART AND CULTURE

That which today would be called the "mark" of this man consisted of an
hereditary ability to define what was beautiful in art and to give it value for
the improvement of the quality of life. If what sociologists say is true, that
the essential element of any political project must be human happiness, Ferdinando, at least on the moral level, did his duty, providing his subjects with
a city on a human scale. The citizens were given the opportunity to benefit
from a stimulating culture of which they could be proud.

Between 1650 and 1660, Ferdinando dedicated himself, along with his
brothers, to the intellectual rebuilding of the state, relaunching the Drawing,
the "Crusca" (for the maintenance of the purity of the Tuscan language), the
"Alterati", the Property and the "Infocati" Academies.

His brother Leopoldo, with his own determined support, created the
"Cimento" Academy in 1657.

In 1656, he had had Ferdinando Tacca build the Pergola Theatre.

He was officially congratulated by the Royal Society, the most important
scientific institute then in existence. This recognition was perhaps made
because of scientific achievements that related back to Galileo, and certainly also because of those of Vincenzo Viviani and Evangelista Torricelli.

When Galileo died on January 8 1642, his body was provisorily buried
in a small room adjacent to the Novitiato Chapel in Santa Croce. The Grand

PIETRO DA CORTONA,
The Golden Age,
1637, Florence, Palatine Gallery,
Stove Room

PIETRO DA CORTONA,
Self-portrait,
circa 1666, Florence, Uffizi

The Little Idol,
first century A.D., Florence,
National Archaeological Museum

Duke had intended to erect a monument to the great scientist but was dissuaded from doing so by opponents who involved Pope Urban VIII in the issue. Galileo would have an honorary burial only in 1737.

In 1637, Ferdinando, a passionate connoisseur of beauty, had had the façade of the Ognisanti Church redone. Three years later, in 1640, he had the equestrian statue of Ferdinando I installed in Piazza Santissima Annunziata.

Giovanni da San Giovanni, along with Francesco Furini, Cecco Bravo and Ottavio Vannini, was commissioned to paint the ground-floor drawing room in the Pitti Palace summer apartment. They created allegorical scenes of the munificence of Laurentian Florence on the walls, and on the ceiling, the allegory of the wedding between Ferdinando and Vittoria. The decoration of the other rooms was entrusted to two painters from Bologna.

But the decisive turning point in the canons of art cultivated up to that time in the city was brought about by Ferdinando's interest in innovation, which stimulated him to break with a certain elegant Florentine mannerism and to interest himself in the Roman baroque work of Pietro da Cortona, whom he asked to decorate the Stove Room in the Pitti Palace winter apartment, in 1637. It was only the beginning: Pietro da Cortona and his student Ciro Ferri also embellished the other public rooms with magnificent decorations. Francesco had received many paintings as part of his wife's dowry, among which were portraits of the Dukes of Urbino by Piero della Francesca, Titian's *Venus* and works by Raphael, in addition to the ancient bronze statue known as *The Little Idol*.

Ferdinando placed the *Hermaphrodite* in the Gallery as well. This work, which he had personally acquired, is one of the most exquisite extant works of ancient sculpture.

TITIAN,
Venus of Urbino,
1538, Florence, Uffizi

With the help of his brothers, he assembled such an impressive collection of paintings that, there being not enough room for them in the Pitti Palace, he was obliged to place some of them in the Uffizi Gallery, effectively tripling the size of the exhibition space. His own portrait, which he had done by Justus Sustermans, is a famous painting that portrays him as almost aggressive and imposing, with the Cross of Grand Master of the Order of Santo Stefano on his chest, in direct contrast to his inherent modesty.

He cultivated a passion for precious objects, which stimulated him to original initiatives such as the setting up of a collection of clocks, jewel boxes, toys, trinkets and accessories decorated with precious stones. He was a methodical collector who could never be accused of dilettantism or randomness in his choices.

PIERO DELLA FRANCESCA,
Diptych of the Dukes of Urbino,
circa 1472, Florence, Uffizi

These are some of the masterpieces which Vittoria della Rovere, the last descendant of the family from Urbino, brought as part of her dowry when she married Ferdinando II in 1631.

COSIMO III
GRAND DUKE

A POLITICALLY MEDIOCRE

FIGURE, HE REDUCED

FLORENCE TO AN ISOLATED

PROVINCE WITH RESPECT TO

THE REST OF EUROPE, WHERE

EVENTS FUNDAMENTAL TO

HISTORICAL, SCIENTIFIC AND

TECHNOLOGICAL

DEVELOPMENT WERE

TAKING PLACE.

FLORENCE 1642
FLORENCE 1723

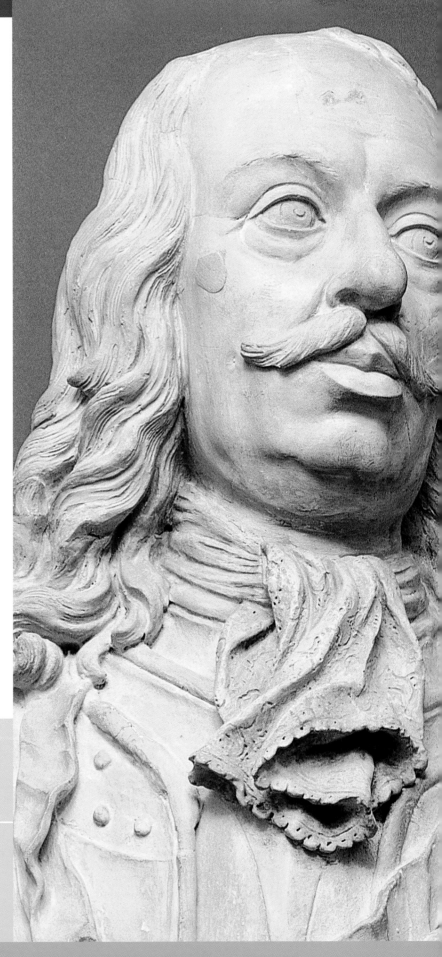

GIOVAN BATTISTA FOGGINI WORKSHOP, *Bust of Cosimo III*, 1723-1725, Florence, Medici Treasures Museum

POLITICAL ROLE

If, from among the Medici who determined the destiny of the family and of Florence, there were those who were good, those who are excellent and those who were bad, Cosimo was undoubtedly a terrible ruler. His reign (1670-1723) was longer than that of his predecessors.

He always acted on the basis of petty and bigoted motives, his character was weak yet he firmly punished and castigated his subjects. As a result of his behaviour, the Grand Duchy lived through a regime of terror that often induced the citizens to malicious gossip, lies, and subterfuge.

Corporal punishment was often inflicted on them and the sentences were carried out in public, so that they should be examples to their fellow citizens. There was, for example, the case of the prostitutes who were stripped nude and whipped after having been accused of having entertained Jews. For this reason, Cosimo III was the first and only Medici who, perhaps because of the influence of certain members of the clergy, was hostile to Jews.

FERDINANDO II ∞ VITTORIA DELLA ROVERE

COSIMO III	∞ MARGUERITE-LOUISE D'ORLEANS

FERDINANDO, ANNA MARIA LUISA AND GIAN GASTONE

He travelled widely throughout the Grand Duchy, but he neither saw nor learned anything, and increasingly engaged himself in imposing compulsory conversion on his own subjects, often in return for cash payments.

He made use of a kind of "public morality" policy, formulated for the most part by priests, which he used in order to spy on families even if they were only suspected of a hypothetical moral offence.

In foreign policy, he demonstrated himself to be extremely cunning, reconciling himself with the Empire in a rather unexpected and sudden way, with the aim of accentuating the conflict between France and Spain. This was clearly not the way to re-establish an autonomous and authoritative Tuscan policy, which had for too long remained outside the world of international politics and, in fact, no longer impressed anyone. The other states recognised very well the inconsistency and low quality of his armed forces. Chronicles from the period, moreover, relate that Cosimo's army was made up of lame soldiers, crippled by the infirmities of old age – some of them being seventy and even eighty years old. He had a miserable fleet of three antiquated galleys moored in the port of Livorno.

And yet, the dramatic conditions under which he lived notwithstanding, Cosimo insisted on receiving royal treatment from the Emperor and, unexpectedly, he succeeded. He, who warranted anything but, was the first Medici to have right to the title of *Supreme Royal Highness*.

Cosimo III became aware that he was facing serious dynastic problems, due to his brother Ferdinando not having had any children. He attempted to avoid the disruptive consequences of the extinction of his dynasty by seeking agreements which would at least guarantee the independence and the form of the state in such a way as to assure its continuity. He was obliged to choose a successor to a family with an illustrious past, a prestigious present and a promising future. It was his intention to provide for his own succession.

In 1713, the problem became more urgent when Ferdinando died, killed by a devastating form of syphilis which had kept him bedridden since 1709, for four tortured years.

At the Utrecht Congress, Cosimo III expressed his intention, its apparently considerable conservatism notwithstanding, to designate his daughter Anna Maria Luisa, Palatine Electress, to succeed Gian Gastone if he should die first.

The agreement was signed in 1714, at which time the powers present did not withhold their assent. However, in 1718, the Empire, France, England and Holland, established with the Treaty of London that the succession to the Grand Duchy of Tuscany was owed to Charles of Bourbon.

Charles, however, preferred to conquer Naples and to become its king as Carlo III. Thus, after many negotiations that took place abroad and in which the family was very involved, Francis Stephen of Lorraine took power when Gian Gastone died.

In spite of the fact that things turned out as they did, Cosimo must be credited for his farsightedness and his attention to preserving Tuscany's autonomy and independence. Tuscany would remain independent, ruled by the Lorraines, and would never become part of the imperial domains, thus maintaining its highly-valued identity.

LUGLIO. / **AGOSTO** / **SETTEMBRE** / **OTTOBRE** / **INVERNO**

ART AND CULTURE

Even though he paid no attention to the development of the arts and sciences, he did have his preferences, such as for the painter Carlo Dolci, and even more for Gaetano Zumbo, who modelled sculptures in wax, often with macabre themes. He had three excellent sculptures brought from Rome, the *Venus*, the *Knifegrinder* and the *Wrestler*, in order to place them in the Uffizi Gallery.

He established the Florentine Academy in Rome, for the training of young Florentine artists, among who were Giovan Battista Foggini and Massimiliano Soldani Berzi.

He particularly interested himself in the interminable work on the Cappella dei Principi. Ferdinando, his son, was more of a connoisseur of art than his father, so much so that, as a collector of Venetian paintings, he was considered the most influential of any of the Medici. With acute intuition, and using his own means, he acquired Raphael's *Madonna with Child and Saints*, Andrea del Sarto's *Madonna of the Harpies* and Parmigianino's *Long-necked Madonna*, as well as Volterrano's *The Joke Played on the*

Priest Arlotto, and exhibited them in Poggio a Caiano, Pratolino and in the Pitti Palace.

Having stayed for some time in Venice, he was fascinated by Venetian painting, contemporary as well as historical, and when he returned to Florence, he asked Sebastiano Ricci to work in the Pitti Palace and in Poggio a Caiano.

In 1706, on the feast day of San Luca, patron saint of painters, Ferdinando had an exhibition of paintings opened in the Santissima Annunziata cloister, and a printed catalogue was prepared for the first time ever.

He was also a sincere and competent admirer of music and literature, which he cultivated according to the family's best traditions.

Ferdinando, however, lived without much affection, because of his

VOLTERRANO,
The Joke Played on the Priest Arlotto,
circa 1640, Florence, Palatine Gallery

father's shyness and of his distance from his mother. Marguerite Louise, bored with court life and absolutely indifferent to her husband, who neglected her, had returned to France and never came back to Florence. Perhaps as a reaction against his father's bigotry and the depressing atmosphere at the court, Ferdinando's public and private behavior seems to have been conspicuously and particularly unbecoming.

LIVIO MEHUS,
Autumn,
Florence, Uffizi

A talented landscape artist, Mehus was among those who benefited from Medici patronage, and provided the grandducal collections with numerous lively and airy works.

Gian Gastone Grand Duke

He was twenty-five years old when he ascended to power. He is another figure whose character it is difficult to describe since he was a fundamentally misanthropic and isolated man.

Florence 1671
Florence 1737

Giovan Battista Foggini Workshop, *Bust of Gian Gastone*, 1723-1725, Florence, Medici Treasures Mus

POLITICAL ROLE

Incapable, like his recent antecedents, of firmly managing power, he attempted to divide it with his sister and with his sister-in-law Violante Beatrice, entrusting to them the tasks inherent in social relationships and in the obligations of court life which they, moreover, were able to carry out brilliantly. He reserved for himself the role of golden recluse that suited him so well.

He thus took advantage of his seclusion in order to follow, undisturbed, his taste for alcohol and for spending most of his time in ambiguous relationships with people of dubious reputation. They were known as the "Ruspanti" because they spent time with him only because they were paid at least one *ruspo* a week (that is, a lilied florin created in Florence by Cosimo III). He was accused of homosexuality and of chronic indulgence and laziness because of his habit of lingering in bed, alone or in company.

Serious doubts about his real inclinations derived from the obstinacy with which his wife insisted on living in Reichstadt in Bavaria, avoiding her husband completely in spite of pressure from both her father and from the Pope himself, who attempted to force her to return to Florence.

And yet, this disturbing individual successfully applied himself to eliminating the abuses which had torn the fabric of Florentine society, getting rid of the spies and of the users of "faith pensions", that is, all the Jews, Turks, and unorthodox Catholics and Protestants who, because of Cosimo III's bigotry, had been paid to convert to the Catholic faith.

Prisoners who had been detained for religious reasons were freed and there were no more public scenes of the disgraceful mockery of the "different".

Finally, he consented to the return of the exiles, obtaining at least their sympathy in recognition.

He died, after much suffering, on July 9 1737.

ART AND CULTURE

Gian Gastone did not die, however, without making a public gesture that was finally worthy of the Medici style. He had a monument to Galileo placed in Santa Croce, a tribute to the man and to science, both of which were to a certain extent vindicated by this act.

The story of the Medici, of their Florence and of their Grand Duchy of Tuscany finishes here, with Gian Gastone and his shadowy life on which, as we have seen, very little light shone.

He was the last of the Medici family, which came to the forefront of Florentine life with Giovanni di Bicci in the early years of the fourteenth century. It had, progressively and almost uninterruptedly, until 1737, determined the destiny of the Florentine state, assuming its de facto government and then constitutionally, through their lineage, its legitimate government. The glorious, enlightened circle had been sadly closed.

COSIMO III ∞ MARGUERITE-LOUISE OF ORLEANS

GIAN GASTONE ∞ ANNA OF SAXONY-LAUENBURG

ANNA MARIA LUISA PALATINE ELECTRESS

THE PALATINE ELECTRESS IS REMEMBERED FOR THE DRAWING UP OF THE "FAMILY PACT" (1737), WHICH ESTABLISHED THE SUCCESSION OF THE HAPSBURG-LORRAINES AND INDISSOLUBLY CONNECTED THE MEDICI TREASURES TO FLORENCE AND TO THE GRAND DUCHY.

FLORENCE 1667
FLORENCE 1743

JAN FRANZ VAN DOUVEN, *Giovanni Guglielmo, Palatine Elector and his wife, Anna Maria Luisa*, circa 171

THE END OF A DYNASTY

THE LAST MEDICI

The last Medici act in favour of Florence, perhaps the most important and most significant act ever carried out by a Medici, was the work of Gian Gastone's sister, the Palatine Electress, Anna Maria Luisa. She donated to the Grand Duchy of Tuscany, in the person of the Grand Duke and his successors, the enormous heritage of works of art, paintings, sculptures and precious objects that filled the family's villas and palaces. Article III of the donation documents place a fundamental condition for the conservation of the treasure: that no object be removed from the total assets and that the collections remain at the complete disposal of all the people of the world, so that everyone could admire them.

THE TREASURE

Essential elements

There follows a summary, incomplete but substantially exhaustive, of the assets left to Tuscany by Maria Luisa. We offer the list to the reader's attention, with the recommendation that the reader make an attentive and considered reflection of the cultural, historical and commercial value of the donation, which consisted of the following extraordinary elements.

All the paintings and all the statues in the Uffizi Gallery, in the Pitti Palace, in the Medici Villa in Rome, and in the other family villas, and which now make up the Florentine museum collections.

COSIMO III ∞ MARGUERITE-LOUISE D'ORLEANS

ANNA MARIA LUISA ∞ JOHAN WILHELM VON DER PFALZ (Palatine Elector)

GRANDDUCAL WORKSHOPS BASED ON
DESIGNS BY GIOVAN BATTISTA FOGGINI,
Palatine Elector's Cabinet,
1709, Florence, Medici Treasures Museum

*Grand Duke Cosimo III gave this cabinet to
his son-in-law. There is a statue of the
Palatine Elector in the centre, surmounted
by the Medici/Pfalz coat of arms.*

GERMAN MANUFACTURE,
*Cameo with portrait
of the Palatine Electress,*
18th century, Florence,
Medici Treasures Museum

An important collection of cameos, carved gems and other similar objects in the Bargello Museum and in the Pitti Palace Medici Treasures Museum. Lorenzo the Magnificent's collection of coins and medals, the oldest such collection in Europe, in the Bargello Museum.

The Sagrestia Nuova, with masterpieces by Michelangelo, and the entire contents of the Medici Library in San Lorenzo.

A large and extremely important collection of Etruscan and Egyptian antiquities which now constitutes the essential nucleus of the Archaeological Museum, in which the Etruscan section is the most prominent.

A precious collection of majolica from Urbino and Faenza, rare armour and curious and valuable weapons, found in the Bargello Museum.

The inlaid tables, the exquisite cabinets and other pieces of furniture, the tapestries and similar objects now in the Pitti, the Uffizi, and the Opificio delle Pietre Dure.

The service of golden fruit, the gold and silver ornaments, the porcelain, the silverware, the pastorals and crucifixes in ivory and amber, the mitre with miniatures made of the plumes of songbirds (which belonged to Clement VII), the reliquaries and other ornaments from the grandducal

First corridor in the Uffizi, Florence

chapel in the Pitti Palace, the splendid niello works, Benvenuto Cellini's beautiful chalices and vases, and many other family objects, now mostly kept in the Pitti Palace and in the Medici chapels.

The immense Medici wardrobe of sumptuous clothing for major ceremonies.

Other treasures joined the Florentine heritage from the Poggio Imperiale villa, from Castello, from Petraia, from Cafaggiolo, from Poggio a Caiano and from all the other Medici residences.

Thus it was that the extraordinary family wealth was able to become first Florentine, then Italian, and then to belong to all of humanity. The people of the world continue to visit the treasures, making the corridors, the gallerys, the rooms and the piazzas of Florence into a global meeting place.

The Medici reigned in Tuscany for approximately three and a half centuries, and very few of them were mediocre. Each one of them, in fact, had strong interests in philosophy, the sciences, art, poetry, music, refined collecting and, in general, in the cult of the beautiful, even if the bloody and overbearing temperament of many of them often qualified them as tyrants.

Their last heir was of similar quality but distinguished herself especially for the generosity with which she made available to us all what anyone who has the opportunity to see it will recognise as the most impressive and glorious collection of unique human expression that has ever been assembled.

Taking Stock of a Dynasty

THE MEDICI

There are so many aspects to this family, to its behaviour, to the role it played in history, to its influence on the development of civilisation as we know it today, that a thorough examination of all its accomplishments would involve a critical analysis that would of necessity be much longer than a merely historiographic one.

The culture that some of the members of the Medici family developed over the centuries had an inestimable impact on European and Occidental civilisation. They made the state of which they were the leaders a powerful force internationally for more than three hundred years. They had defining influence on art, poetry, architecture, aesthetic taste in general, and on the sciences. They influenced the development of the way of thinking in the times in which they lived, facilitating the passage from Renaissance humanism to the Enlightenment, and therefore to the modern age as we now understand it. The judgement of history and the image of the Medici family that it offers us today as an icon of the collective imagination are to be read, from the critical viewpoint, as a willing sacrifice to the intellect. Ultimately, the form of a cult (which seems to exist only as an indigenous phenomenon).

The development of Florence is indissolubly connected to the Medici's actions, behaviour, and politics, but also to their temperament and to their interests. It would certainly not be possible, in fact it would be anti-historical, to imagine a hypothesis different from that which the leadership shown by this family accomplished in the development of the city, compared to the other major families over which they prevailed. Neither is it possible to imagine which objectives civilisation might have reached if, instead of being carried along by the direct and rapid river of the Medici family, it had been borne along by an irregular and turbulent current, represented by one of the other many alternative possibilities.

This family was comprised of individuals who were contradictory and disturbing, brilliant and perverse, fantastical and shrewd, generous and base, luminous and obscure. Not even the personality of a unique Prince such as Lorenzo the Magnificent is without the perverse play of light and shadow

OTTAVIO VANNINI,
Lorenzo in the Midst of Artists,
1635-1642, Florence, Medici Treasures Museum, Giovanni da San Giovanni Room

In the fresco, the painter portrays the outstanding patron Lorenzo the Magnificent with a group of artists, among which is Michelangelo showing one of his first works, a bust of an ancient-style faun, now lost.

Medici genealogical tree,
1699, Florence,
Medici Treasures Museum

which touched all the members of this family. Lorenzo, to whom are owed the major splendours of this model City-state, realised principally by means of the recovery and reintroduction of classical values and the restitution of the centrality of the individual, is known also to have behaved contemptibly and shamefully. Acts of frightening and vengeful violence are attributed to him – such as his compliance with the so-called sack of Volterra, and his fury against the Pazzi after the assassination of his brother Giuliano – as well as dissolute and licentious behaviour. Sixtus IV explicitly accused him of cultivating a perverse tendency to tyranny. Nevertheless, Lorenzo, an eminent figure in this exceptional family, was considered the worthiest man who had ever held the reins of a state. Without him the history of Florence would not have been written in the same way.

Lorenzo synthesises the concept of the Renaissance, which would later develop through the work and thinking of his successors. Moreover, he influenced the development of the culture that would follow him, because of the extraordinary importance of the ideas of Marsilio Ficino and Pico della Mirandola, ideas that he shared and spread. The latter, gifted with an exceptional mind and character, had the courage to present himself in Rome, at the age of only twenty-four years, with a list of nine hundred philosophical, cabalistic and theological texts. Condemned for heresy, he was saved by Lorenzo the Magnificent, who had the condemnation revoked. With reference to Lorenzo, Fred Bérence expresses the following opinion of one of Lorenzo's particular merits: "the real miracle was that he believed in other men, that he valued them almost absolutely, often offering them the supreme opportunity to be those who go against the laws, the groups and the people who represent perversity. He also made it possible for artists, whose only refuge in other situations would have been desperation, to live and work".

THE THEORY OF A DEVELOPMENT

Humanism, Renaissance and Enlightenment

The rediscovery of human reason and of its eternal universality was the result of a philosophical development the roots of which are found in the individual's claim to an earthly and secular existence, which constituted the very essence of humanism and of the Renaissance and which facilitated an autonomous vision of the phenomenon, one which could induce in mankind a profoundly new way of thinking. This was understood by only a few thinkers, such as D'Alembert who, when presenting his *Encyclopaedia* in 1751, expressed thanks to the Italian Renaissance for having given humanity "the sciences, the fine arts and good taste, and innumerable models of incomparable perfection".

Such a flattering opinion draws attention to an essential aspect of the question. Humanism appeared to be a primarily literary movement in which philosophy, at the beginning, was only indirectly involved, as a part of Greco-Roman culture. It would be more correct to add that the recovery of the individual as the interpreter of his own destiny was theoretically predominant, but that aesthetics had much more importance, in terms of the completeness of the system, like in Pico's famous *De dignitate homini*.

It was this aspect of Neoplatonic thought that stimulated the Renaissance Florentine man to give maximum value to beauty, rendering it sublime, in abstract intellectual evaluations as well in the construction of a city of dreams, flooded with music and poetic songs, where magnificence, taste and creativity in every branch of the arts were expressed at levels never again reached.

This occurred, also and especially, because of the constant participatory passion of the Medici family, naturally inclined to promote its own image by means of the innumerable masterpieces that it habitually commissioned with a discerning use of its affluence.

SEBASTIANO RICCI,
Medici Coat of Arms,
1707, Florence, Pitti Palace,
ground-floor room

MEDICI MEMORIES

Italy, divided up into small states that were as glorious as they were unrealistic, and conditioned by the unique, organic and centralist power of the Church of Rome, had, with the Medici, the most important reigning family spanning the Middle Ages, the Renaissance and the modern age. And yet Florence did not elevate this family to the prominence which it deserved, nor did it a make it into a national icon with the image of superiority of which it was worthy.

If, as appears to be the case, this is true, it is due to many possible reasons. For example, the reluctance shown by the Florentines to share with others the glory they had always considered as belonging integrally and only to them; the Medici family, to whatever extent it was the supreme expression of the city, was always also a part of that city. The prevalence of intellectual and artistic achievements over military and territorial concerns, with the consequent supremacy of the courtier over the condottiere, led to the feeling that the Medici court was more exceptional than its practically non-existent and nearly always mercenary army was glorious.

Although scholars have disagreed, and still disagree, concerning their evaluations of the Medici, the more accredited opinions agree on two points: the splendour and the intellectual genius of most of the representatives of the family and the legitimacy of the exceptional results that they were able to attain. The city of Florence itself is a concentration of all the glorious achievements of the Medici who – apart from the presence in Rome of the Medici pontiffs and what has remained in Rome as a consequence of their presence there and of the commissions made by Leo X and Clement VII – worked for centuries to make Florence an ideal place. A place the nature of which, when it was achieved, was that of a superb normality, derived from the extemporaneousness of a form of behaviour that was always consistent with the personal interests of the head of the family at any given time.

Florence and the Medici are characterised by the reciprocity of their love-hate relationship, and the memories which have resulted belong first to the Florentines and then to the rest of the world. This is not a question of provincialism but, on the contrary, of an exclusive pride in this exceptional family. The Florentines claimed the Medici for themselves. The family had made its presence felt throughout Europe, it had interacted with its monarchies, it had influenced its palaces and customs and it had always, with great skill, or perhaps unconsciously, returned to Florence what it had offered to the world.

A METHOD, A REASON

The story of an illustrious family is the sum of many profiles. The way these profiles are assembled defines the unitary effect that is the first requirement of any narrated event, so that the story may be imitable in the Baconian sense, and therefore pleasing to the potential reader, who is hopefully curious to learn how it will end. The lives of the family members, if written about with diligence and taste, and with the intention of representing people whose actions, both large and small, both public and private, are blended together, ideally results in a lively and accurate representation, and is thus more inspiring of imitation. Gilbert Burnet wrote the following interpretation of Bacon's thesis, which is indeed very germane: "[...] The lives of heroes and princes are often full of accounts of their great achievements, which belong to a general rather than to a particular story and entertain the reader's imagination with a splendid unfolding of greatness [...]".

To write a family's biography is a work of serial portraiture in which it is difficult to focus on individual figures since such a biography must respond to the need so clearly expressed by Montaigne when he maintains that, in biographies, "[...] the sense of the human in the very movement of the personal reality observed as closely as possible [...]" is to be sought for, in a kind of triumph of the individual, who becomes a Renaissance man only because of the fact of being the centre of attention. The requirements of synthesis, in our case, and of the modest horizon which has been our context, have hopefully resulted in the depiction of facets of the impressive whole represented by the Medici. The family monument which is the Medici identity is a vast entity the unitary spirit of which is perhaps represented by three excesses: too aesthetically famous, too ethically despised, too meanly envied.

Detail of the terracotta floor
in the Medici-Laurentian Library
Reading Room, Florence

Printed in August 2002
by
Genesi, Città di Castello (Pg)
for
s i l l a b e